The Quotable Baseball Fanatic

Books by Louis D. Rubin, Jr.

Babe Ruth's Ghost
Before the Game *(photographs by Scott Mylin)*
Black Poetry in America *(with Blyden Jackson)*
The Curious Death of the Novel
The Edge of the Swamp
The Even-Tempered Angler
The Faraway Country
A Gallery of Southerners
George W. Cable: A Biography
The Golden Weather: A Novel
The Heat of the Sun: A Novel
The Mockingbird in the Gum Tree
No Place on Earth
Seaports of the South *(with J. F. Harrington)*
Small Craft Advisory
Surfaces of a Diamond: A Novel
The Teller in the Tale
Thomas Wolfe: The Weather of His Youth
Virginia: A Bicentennial History
The Wary Fugitives
William Elliott Shoots a Bear
The Writer in the South

The Quotable Baseball Fanatic

COMPILED BY
LOUIS D. RUBIN, JR.

FOREWORD BY
ROY BLOUNT, JR.

Main Street
A division of Sterling Publishing Co., Inc.
New York

Library of Congress Cataloging-in-Publication Data available

10 9 8 7 6 5 4 3 2 1

Published by Main Street, a division of Sterling Publishing Co., Inc.
387 Park Avenue South, New York, NY 10016

Distributed in Canada by Sterling Publishing
c/o Canadian Manda Group, One Atlantic Avenue, Suite 105
Toronto, Ontario, Canada M6K 3E7
Distributed in Great Britain by Chrysalis Books Group PLC
The Chrysalis Building, Bramley Road, London W10 6SP, England
Distributed in Australia by Capricorn Link (Australia) Pty. Ltd.
P.O. Box 704, Windsor, NSW 2756, Australia

Sterling ISBN   1-4027-1425-4

For Bob Creamer

Contents

Foreword

The other day a fact-checker at a magazine called to ask whether the statement "Baseball is a game where people sit around and spit and say stupid things" should, in fact, be attributed to me. Loath as I am to disclaim being the first person to say almost anything, I said no. I did vaguely recall having quoted Bill Lee, the former Red Sox pitcher (that he was a pitcher should go without saying, but you can't say "the former Red Sock"), as having been quoted in the seventies as saying, when asked what he thought about artificial grass, "I don't know, I never smoked any"—that observation had a certain cogency. Coming from a writer, it would be inappropriate. Making clever remarks is not a ballplayer's primary imperative. Before he has any room to talk, he has to speak with bat, ball, fingers, and feet. And yet a player's tongue is often mightier than the pen.

In 1988, when David Cone was a young Met pitcher about to start a crucial playoff game, a more experienced teammate (I'm sorry to say my archives do not record his name) was asked what advice he had given Cone. "There's no magical saying," said the teammate. "There's nothing we can say except he can't look at it like, 'Oh, my God, the earth will crash if I don't do it.' If he realizes the situation too much, that's not good."

That, to me, is wisdom. You have to choose between fully realizing a situation and performing well in it. Or, as Yogi Berra is famously supposed to have said, "You can't think and hit at the same time." Ask anyone who has just pitched a no-hitter or hit a dramatic game-winning home run what the experience was like, and he will tell you, if he is honest, "It hasn't sunk in yet." You have to be a little bit unconcious out there. As Reggie Jackson once said, "When the ball is in the air and it starts hopping, all you can do is follow with your eyes and sing along."

When a ballplayer does come up with an epigram regarding his own play, it likely pertains to poor performance. Once when Reggie was hitting .175, he said, "When you're hitting

.175, whatever you say doesn't make much sense." In fact, paradoxically enough, he thereby struck the verbal ball right on the nose. In 1974, when Reggie was at the height of his powers, he sloshed around in the whirlpool bath in the Oakland clubhouse and searched for words to describe what hitting well is like:

"Being in complete control. *You* have been the dominant force—not the ball, not the pitcher. You have taken over and *lined* it somewhere." And when the ball goes a long, long ways, "All the baseball players come to rest at that moment and watch you. Everyone is helpless and in awe. . . . And you know it. You're a master. *Dealing.*"

Eloquent in its way, but too far from the general experience of life to have the resonance of something Reggie said in his last season, when asked why he was considering retirement: "I don't want to go on wringing out the rag of ability."

Ballplayers live in a physical world. Joe Morgan is an estimable TV commentator today, but none of his reflections on the fine points of the game have registered with me as distinctly as something he told me once in his prime as a Cincinnati Red, after he hit a line drive into the gap and beat the outfielder's throw to second by sliding headfirst. "That's the only way I can slide on a double," he said. "Because I be in a deep lean."

Canted profoundly forward, that's the way a ballplayer has to be. Acting on faith. Thinking positively, which is not to say scintillatingly. During spring training in 1981 George Foster, newly acquired by the Mets, would respond to questions about the team's prospects by holding his hand over the 5 of the 15 on his chest so that his shirt read "Mets 1." That, he said, was his goal: "If you have a goal, you achieve only twenty percent." Which must mean, a cynical sportswriter observed, that "if you do and you don't, you must achieve a hundred percent." The latter was the sharper remark, but it was also the remark of a man who was not in a deep lean. If you are a ballplayer you do *or* you don't. Then, somewhat later, you may descend to the level of words.

—Roy Blount, Jr.

Introduction

In the days of John J. McGraw, when it was considered great to be young and a New York Giant, there was an umpire named William J. Byron. Known variously as "Hummingbird," "Lord Byron," and "Singing Bill," he was a poet and a good baseball man. It was Byron who, while umpiring in the minors, advised the Detroit Tigers to sign young Tyrus Raymond Cobb.

In 1913 Byron began a seven-year tenure as a member of the National League's umpiring staff. Whenever he made a call that did not meet with the approval of McGraw and the Giants manager came storming from the dugout to express his disagreement, as frequently he did, Byron would burst into song. "Here comes McGraw!" he sang, to the tune of the Wedding March from "A Midsummer Night's Dream."

It was Byron's practice sometimes to accompany his decisions on balls and strikes with poetic advice to the batter.

"You'll have to learn before you're older / You can't hit the ball with the bat on your shoulder," he might declare; or, "It cut the middle of the plate / You missed because you swung too late." Whether his verse was composed on the spur of the moment, or whether it was prepared in advance and applied as occasion arose, is not known, at least not to me.

I cite the above in order to make two points about the book of quotations that follows. They may be best put in the form of questions:

1. In what other team sport is a participant permitted and even expected to make regular visits to the playing field to dispute the judgment of the officials, bringing the game to a complete halt while doing so?

2. How many officials of professional football or basketball games that took place even ten years ago, much less three-quarters of a century, can one identify by name and tell funny stories about?

As must be obvious to all sports fans who do much reading, a great deal that is memorable and interesting about the game of baseball centers on the cultivation of personalities. As Tom Boswell once wrote, "We pretend baseball is primarily a game of teams, when it's more about people. Ted Williams played in only one World Series; Walter Johnson, Hank Aaron and Rogers Hornsby in two each. Who cares or remembers? The team may be the individual's context, but its success is not its definition." What we watch are the members of the teams as they take their separate turns on center stage.

In professional basketball, a sport that requires great skill to play, complex teamwork and split-second screening and positioning are essential to success. Yet unless we happen to be especially experienced observers and at all times know just where to look, most of what we see during a game consists of swift passes and a melee of moving bodies, followed by a Michael Jordan gracefully placing the ball inside the hoop. Contrast that with the spectacle of a pitcher standing in isolation on the mound, getting ready to resume action, taking the sign from the catcher, preparing to throw; and a batter stepping into the box, setting his feet, cocking his wrists and adjusting the hold on his bat, waiting for the pitch. Will it be low and away, in on the fists, or high and outside? Will it be a fastball, a curve, a slider, a changeup? Will it be thrown for a strike, or wasted? There is ample time to observe and antici-pate.

The venting of emotion, as noted, is an important part of the spectacle. Those participating are encouraged to sound off. Most of us who have watched televised NFL football games have seen brief footage of this or that coach raging away at a head linesman along the sidelines, while the head linesman totally ignores what is being shouted at him as he prepares for the next play. Let that coach become so irate that he ventures upon the field itself and holds up play, however, and heads will roll, for it is strictly taboo. This may be com-pared with a Bobby Cox or a Lou Piniella furiously disputing a call at second base, passionately gesturing, the center of all attention, play having been suspended to permit the argu-ment to go on, while the fans in the grandstand are vigorously expressing their own opinions. The difference in conduct and mores is beyond dispute.

To that, add the number of baseball games played during a season, the number of separate appearances in action, and the number of years in which a good player can remain in public view, and it is not difficult to see why the sport is dominated by its personalities, and why the antics of individuals are so much a part of the game and its history. This is why we remember, and can quote so specifically, what has been said by and about them, and about the game they play.

The book that follows is based on that fundamental fact, and is made up of comments by persons who have been involved in professional baseball, whether as participants, commentators, or simply as spectators. Some are humorous, others not so. I do not say that a similar book might not be assembled from sayings and writings about other major sports, but surely there would be many fewer quotations from which to choose.

There is a famous comment by F. Scott Fitzgerald to the effect that Ring Lardner's muse was permanently constrained by the boundaries of Frank Chance's diamond, the implication being that had Lardner not spent his formative years covering baseball in Chicago and listening to the conversations of athletes, the fiction he later wrote would have been more ambitious, of greater range, and more richly imaginative—i.e., more like Fitzgerald's.

Jonathan Yardley, for one, has disputed this, on the grounds that no good purpose was served by trying to make

Lardner into a different and supposedly more artistically ennobled kind of writer than what he so felicitously was. Surely this is true. The real question is not whether Lardner might have written to greater literary purpose if he had spent his late teens and early twenties in an environment offering greater intellectual stimulation than a dugout or a press box. It is why the game of baseball could exercise so powerful a hold on his youthful imagination, and in the particular form that it did.

Whatever the reasons, it cannot be denied that major league baseball has engaged the attention of a number of very talented writers. It would appear to provide, for some of them, a kind of bridge between what is intellectually and artistically sophisticated on the one hand, and what is exciting and appealing to a mass general audience on the other. I do not mean by this that the other major sports have no appeal for the intelligentsia; clearly they do. But for whatever reason, when the urge to write about such things comes along, it is usually baseball that they choose to write about.

I sometimes think that no small portion of the fascination of reading about baseball arises from the contrast between the way in which the game is written about by its literary admirers, and the way it is talked about by its player personnel. This is particularly true for humor. If, as has been maintained, incongruity is what lies at the root of all comedy, then consider the difference in levels of discourse displayed in so much that appears in this book. It may be seen beginning with the first section, entitled "The Nature of the Game." Whose insight comes closer to the unadulterated truth about the innermost nature of the National Game, the noted former practitioner Yogi Berra's, or the distinguished philosopher Morris R. Cohen's? The answer, of course, is that both comments are much to the point.

Baseball players can be and frequently are very witty. With only very rare exceptions, however, they display their wit in conversation, not on paper. When their names appear on book jackets, it is habitually in company with someone else's, "as told to," or "with" another person; in other words, the books are the work of ghostwriters.

"As told to" books are principally aimed at the young adult audience, and one can never be sure that the ballplayer actually said or even thought what he has supposedly written.

Most such books are eminently forgettable. Not so the first-person memoirs of a relatively new sub-genre invented by Lawrence Ritter and since practiced by Donald Honig, Anthony Connor, Daniel Peary, and numerous others. What Ritter had the inspiration to do, back in the 1960s, was to track down and interview a number of oldtime ballplayers, and develop their spoken memories into first-person sketches. At the time he did this, not only were some of the stars of the Dead Ball Era still around, but even a few who had played the game professionally back before the turn of the twentieth century.

The Glory of Their Times is a deceptive book. So skillfully have the random and sometimes discordant replies of the old-timers been woven into seamless narratives that a reader might think that Ritter did little more than take down their recollections. In actuality it is Ritter who provides most of the development, the cohesion and the continuity. Not all his emulators have been as successful.

Some of the very best writing about baseball is in biographies: Robert Creamer's Stengel, Murray Polner's Branch Rickey, Peter Williams on Bill Terry's career, and so on.

Columnists such as George F. Will and Thomas Boswell likewise produce felicitous prose, the best of which has been collected and published, while Roger Angell's extensive *New Yorker* commentaries are imaginative and frequently eloquent.

On the other hand, a great deal of baseball writing is flat, sterile stuff, composed on the stylistic level of the Horatio Alger tales. For every craftsman of the language such as Roger Kahn and Leonard Koppett, there are numerous authors of baseball books which read as if their prose was bolted into place on an assembly line. Some of the worst baseball writing comes from the "as told to" books written for the young-adult trade, which seek to convey the impression that the ballplayer himself is actually doing the writing through attempting to counterfeit his vocabulary, four-letter words and all. I could quote examples, but it would be too depressing. Still, ghostwriting can be also spritely and deft, as witness the job that Ed Linn did for and on Leo Durocher in *Nice Guys Finish Last.*

In part, the liveliness of a baseball book depends upon the particular subject matter. Obviously an author who writes of Casey Stengel or Ty Cobb has an inherent advantage over one who chronicles Joe DiMaggio or Rogers Hornsby, in that the latter two, for all their talent with a baseball bat, have little to offer in the way of personality. DiMaggio was aloof and inchoate, while Hornsby was a sourpuss, and a biographer's language can do only so much to atone for a subject's lack of color. Even so, writers choose their own subjects, and those with a feel for prose tend to write books about interesting ballplayers. It is also a fact that an extremely useful qualification for writing baseball books is a sense of humor, which unfortunately not all who have done so possess.

To select the quotations that make up this book, I read, or more usually reread, several hundred books, and picked the brains of various knowledgeable acquaintances. I tried, so far as was possible, to avoid some of the more time-worn quotations, such as Ping Bodie's announcement that he roomed with Babe Ruth's suitcase, or Dizzy Dean's comment that if he had known that his brother Paul was going to pitch a no-hitter, he would have done the same, and the like. On the other hand, I could not bring myself to leave out, for example, Bugs Baer on Bodie's feet being more law-abiding than his intentions, and sometimes I deliberately included a platitude because it was and is so obviously that. Thus I cited Jacques Barzun's oft-quoted comment about whoever would know the mind and heart of America needing to study baseball, which is so regularly invoked in order to justify the importance of a game that needs no justification. As well contend that whoever would know the mind and heart of America must know peanut butter.

Writing and thinking about baseball is always subject to the temptations of nostalgia. Not only is the game played during one's childhood and youth, and thus recollected with the fondness for a period when the future still appeared open for the taking, but the time for playing and watching baseball was usually the summertime, when school was out and the sky high and blue. For this and other reasons the Good Old Days, and the resulting legend of Decline and Fall, have constituted a thriving dimension of the game for more than a century now. The seemingly valid specificity and continuity of baseball statistics, as contrasted with those of other sports, helps to feed the myth of the Golden Age. How could even the best of today's pitchers compare favorably with a Christy Mathewson, who won 37 games, with an earned-run average of 1.43, and completed 34 games in 1908? The fact that the statistics are only relatively comparable, and that there are a number of reasons why pitching major league baseball is a far more difficult affair today, matters little when viewed through the lens of the Search for Lost Time.

Just when the Golden Age was at its zenith depends upon one's own antiquity. Not many old timers have the objectivity of Wilbert Robinson when asked to compare the New York Yankees of the 1920s with the fabled Orioles of the 1890s. "They would have kicked the hell out of us," Uncle Robbie declared, to the indignation of John McGraw and others of his old Baltimore teammates.

One of the earliest pieces about baseball that I read was by Robert Benchley, in a collection of his magazine pieces entitled *Love Conquers All* (1922). I read it in the mid-1930s. Benchley was suggesting, facetiously, that baseball fans should have a distinctive dress, as follows: "Straw hat, worn well back on the head; one cigar, unlighted, held between teeth; vest worn but unbuttoned and open, displaying both a belt and suspenders, with gold watchchain connecting the bottom pockets."

Obviously the fan is wearing a suit, with a vest, and almost nobody would dress so formally and cumbrously for baseball games any more. Pocket watches and chains have virtually disappeared, in favor of wristwatches. Suspenders are for the most part long gone. It is taboo to smoke cigars in public, and nobody would buy one at today's prices merely to chew on it. The straw hat alone remains valid, and then only for some. Moreover, it was Benchley's assumption that a baseball fan was by definition male; another sketch in the same collection contains a humorous portrayal of the sufferings of a husband who makes the mistake of taking his wife along to a Yankees game. She cannot understand, for example, why a baserunner coming home does not constitute a home run.

So the comedy in Benchley's piece, based as it is on "typical" diamond-watching garb as popularly portrayed in the early 1920s, is almost totally outdated. But what was taking place not in the grandstand but out on the playing field then has in most respects changed very little. As A. Bartlett Giamatti has said, the game's rules were established, "with almost no exceptions of consequence, by 1895." In essence, its fundamentals do remain the same.

Thus, what Burleigh Grimes, one of the last of the legal spitballers, quotes Rogers Hornsby coming out to the mound and telling him at a crucial point of a game played some seven decades ago could be spoken by any manager of any era: "Don't give him anything good, but don't walk him." And the perennially unfeeling ways of numerous bleacherites toward once-lustrous veterans grown old and slow were amply summed up by a comment made to me by a spectator at a minor league game in Baltimore 47 years ago. "Baseball fans," he remarked, "have short memories. I've even seen them boo Walter Johnson, and in my opinion he was the greatest pitcher who ever lived."

The fans too can be long-suffering, however. It was so in Mudville, and in Cleveland, Chicago, Atlanta, Boston and everywhere else that the game has been played. I once did a tabulation designed to indicate which major league city's fans have suffered most and least over the years, in the way of having to get by without home teams in the pennant races. Counting the annual records of all but the most recent franchises, I found, not surprisingly, that from 1901 through the 1995 season a baseball fan living in New York City was most likely to have a local team finish the season fewer than ten games out of the running. By contrast, a fan living in Philadelphia, whether rooting for the Phillies or, before 1955, the Athletics, was least apt of all to have enjoyed such a privilege—less so, even, than a citizen of Chicago.

Still, pain can be inflicted by any ball team anywhere upon its adherents. I doubt that a more difficult time, more demanding of fortitude and calling for greater spiritual resolve, was ever endured than was true for partisans of the then-New York Giants on the day, midway through the 1948 season, when the news came that Mel Ott had been fired as manager and Leo Durocher hired in his stead. By definition all Giant fans adored Ott. Contrariwise, they did not merely dislike Leo; they hated him with a passion. It was Leo who had snarled and cursed and hustled the Dodgers along to hegemony among National League teams in New York City following almost forty years of Giant dominance. It was he who had pointed to Mel Ott and the Giants and declared that nice guys finished last. Ottie was a gentleman, Durocher a barroom brawler, crude and mannerless. And now he, of all people, was being placed in charge of the Giants!

The New York papers were full of the news. The views of various fans were solicited. There were those patrons of the Polo Grounds who declared that this was the end. They could take no more. They were cancelling lifelong allegiances. It was a fan of the Brooklyn Dodgers, however, who came up with what to my mind was one of the classic baseball utterances of all time. I have remembered it ever since. "Jeez!" he declared. "It's Poil Harbor for da Giants!" Yet as it turned out, the Polo Grounds regulars were soon to relent, and three seasons later Leo's Giants won the pennant.

The book that follows divides roughly into two parts. The first consists of comments appropriate to certain general topics and attitudes, as for example the Nature of the Game, the Good Old Days, the art of catching, the end of the color line, sports writers, and so on. The second part contains remarks about or by various players of the game. Little attempt has been made to "cover" all the best-known or most representative players. While at work on this book I focused on finding piquant comments rather than any treatment of particular subjects. The groupings came afterward. Some may wonder why, for example, there are two pages of quotations having to do with Ty Cobb, but none about Harry Heilman or Al Simmons. It is because I don't know of, and didn't in my readings happen to come across, striking comments by or about either of the latter two gentlemen, remarkable though their hitting skills were, while almost everybody had something to say, frequently derogatory, about the Georgia Peach.

So it goes in what has been described as "the temple of baseball," but that to my mind has always seemed more like a high-quality three-ring circus.

L. D. R.

Chapel Hill, North Carolina
May 11, 1999

The Quotable Baseball Fanatic

1

The Nature of the Game

Some Observations, Philosophical and Otherwise . . .

Brains are as much a necessity in base-ball as in any other profession. The best ball players are the most intelligent, though, of course, natural intelligence is here meant and not necessarily that which is derived from books.

JOHN MONTGOMERY WARD (1888)

Critics who spurn baseball as slow and tranquil, out of step with the violence which mars our times, fail to grasp its enormous impact on the masses. Baseball's solitary grace is not obscured in a bedlam of bodies, or in a jarring crash near the goal, or in a madcap scramble near the backboard. Its grace exists to be seen, not clouded, and those who excel on the field or in the broadcast booth magnify that artistry.

CURT SMITH

The anatomical ideal of the wedge-shaped athlete, broad in the shoulder and slim hipped, is an artist's generalization, which we owe to ancient Greece. When a great player appears with a different form—Yogi Berra, Honus Wagner, Babe Ruth—people think him deformed.

MARSHALL SMELSER

It takes us out of outer chaos, removes us from the formless worldly confusion, and conveys us to a set arena, formal and precise. We're placed square in a well-defined system that renders visible, actual, palpable, each and every varied mystery that happens under its rules. Its universe is well-timed and orderly.

MARVIN COHEN

The ball is in motion. The ball lives. The players? Mere adjuncts.

MARVIN COHEN

I love baseball too much to do anything else. When the season is over I'm grouchy all the time. I feel miserable. I'm always sick. I get imaginary pains, like a baby. Only when spring training comes around and I can put the uniform back on do the pains go away.

WOODY HUYKE

When my revered friend and teacher William James wrote an essay on "A Moral Equivalent for War," I suggested to him that baseball already embodied all the moral value of war, so far as war had any moral value. He listened sympathetically and was amused, but he did not take me seriously enough. All great men have their limitations, and William James's were due to the fact that he lived in Cambridge, a city which, in spite of the fact that it has a population of 100,000 souls (including the professors), is not represented in any baseball league that can be detected without a microscope.

MORRIS R. COHEN

———————

Two weeks in a hand-ball court will put a team in better condition to begin a season than any Southern trip, and in the end be less expensive to the club.

JOHN MONTGOMERY WARD (1888)

The desert sun hammered down on us, casting rocklike shadows on the infield and softer shapes on the thick green grass of the outfield, but there was a warm breeze blowing out toward center field and beyond, where a little windmill spun and glittered in the sunshine. In the stands we yelled happily and almost impartially, admiring the ballplayers and the close, meaningless, money-free game, not wanting it to end.

ROGER ANGELL

Before a game in St. Louis in 1955, Russ [Meyer] was sitting alone in the Dodgers dugout. He picked up an old baseball, looked at it carefully, and said, speaking to himself and to no one:

"Just think of it. This little ball causes all of the trouble."

JAMES T. FARRELL

Midsummer baseball feels as if it would last forever; late-season baseball becomes quicker and terser, as if sensing its coming end, and sometimes, if we are lucky, it explodes into brilliant terminal colors, leaving bright pictures in memory to carry us through the miserable months to come.

ROGER ANGELL

For someone whose roots in America were strong but only inches deep, and who had no experience, such as a Catholic child might, of an awesome hierarchy that was real and felt, baseball was a kind of secular church that reached into every class and region of the nation and bound millions upon millions of us together in common concerns, loyalties, rituals, enthusiasms, and antagonisms. Baseball made me understand what patriotism was about, at its best.

PHILIP ROTH

As a boy I had gone to a school that was run by the Catholic Church and was intended to direct kids to the seminary. So religion had been part of my background. At first Ron Northey—who was trying to make it back into the majors—called me "Reverend." When I told him I didn't like that, he changed it to "Professor." I said, "That's insulting to a lot of bright men in academia." But the name stuck.

JIM BROSNAN

I claim that Base Ball owes its prestige as our National Game to the fact that as no other sport it is the exponent of American Courage, Confidence, Combativeness; American Dash, Discipline, Determination; American Energy, Eagerness, Enthusiasm; American Pluck, Persistency, Performance; American Spirit, Sagacity, Success; American Vim, Vigor, Virility.

ALBERT G. SPALDING

Genteel in its origins, proletarian in its development, egalitarian in its demands and appeal, effortless in its adaptation to nature, raucous, hard-nosed, and glamorous as a profession, expanding with the country like fingers unfolding from a fist, image of a lost past, evergreen reminder of America's best promises, baseball fits America.

A. BARTLETT GIAMATTI

It ain't like football. You can't make up no trick plays.

YOGI BERRA

It's great to be young and a Giant.

LARRY DOYLE

It's great to be young and a Yankee.

WAITE HOYT

If you became a Yankee, you took on the quality of breeding which the Yankees exemplified. You became a Yankee, and that answered a whole lot of questions. For some reason you were able to perform a little better.

WAITE HOYT

Of all the teams I played on, the Yankees were the team that drank the most.

JOE DE MAESTRI

With exceptions like Oakland and the pennant-winning Yankee teams I played on (where there was more dissention than on my last-place Seattle Pilots), winning teams tend to have less dissention because players having good years are generally happier. Dissention is the result, rather than the cause, of losing.

JIM BOUTON

Everyone is aware of the Calvinist nature, the sense of foreboding that attaches itself to the Red Sox.

ROGER ANGELL

Baseball isn't a life-and-death matter, but the Red Sox are.

MIKE BARNICLE

Those Dodger-Giant games weren't baseball. They were civil war.

ANDY PAFKO

2

The Good Old Days

Back When Baseball Was Baseball . . .

I have read so much about the old-timers and heard older players and writers and fans (including my father) talk about them so often that they are almost as visible to me as the stars I have watched on the field.

ROGER ANGELL

Baseball was a neater and tidier game before the First World War than it was after. The single run had more value because it was harder to get with the old dead ball. When [Babe] Ruth came to play, batters were hitting well below their averages of the 1890s.

MARSHALL SMELSER

Whenever the ball is caught after rebounding from the side of a building, a fence, or a tree, provided it has touched the ground but once, it should be considered a fair catch, unless a special arrangement to the contrary be made previous to the commencement of the match. This rule will also hold good in the case of a catch without touching the ground at all.

SEYMOUR R. CHURCH (1902)

In fact, "modern" baseball ought to be dated not from the beginning of the twentieth century, as popular lore confidently assumes, but from the season of 1893. Under the new rules, the pitching distance was lengthened from fifty feet to sixty feet, six inches; the rectangular pitcher's box was eliminated; and, as he delivered the ball to the batter, the pitcher was required to keep his back foot anchored to a twelve-by-four rubber slab (enlarged to twenty-four by six inches in 1895.)

The results were everything the rule-makers could have desired. The 1893 season brought the sharpest increase in batting figures in the sport's history: a thirty-five-point rise in the overall National League average and almost a thousand more runs.

CHARLES C. ALEXANDER

Names like Whitey, Hoss, Brickyard, Dapper Dan, and Big Bill are easily understood, and we can guess how Benny (Earache) Meyer earned his designation. We can guess why Dirty Jack Doyle played for twelve different teams in seventeen years, too. Since he won 203 games, Al Orth (1895–1909) probably didn't mind being called "the Curveless Wonder," but what did Bill Lattimore do in his four-game stay with the 1908 Cleveland club to earn the title "Slothful Bill"? And how, in God's name, did Hub Perdue, of the Boston Braves and St. Louis Cardinals (1911–15) come to be called "the Gallatin Squash"*?

ART HILL

[* ans.—because he came from Gallatin and was shaped like a squash.—ed.]

3

Losers

And Some Get Rained Out . . .

Of the sixteen teams that existed in 1949, all have since won league championships—all but the Cubs. And which of the old National League teams was first to finish in tenth place behind even the expansion teams? Don't ask.

GEORGE F. WILL

For consistency, Philadelphia has always been the worst. In nine years during Pat's tenure at the old Baker Bowl and Shibe Park, both the Phillies and the A's finished in last place.

JIMMY BRESLIN

One dreary afternoon [in the 1930s], Dave Driscoll, business manager of the Dodgers, was walking in Philadelphia and chanced to pass Baker Bowl. The Phillies were on the road, but in spite of that a pathetic vendor of peanuts was hawking his wares before an imaginary crowd near the entrance to the bleachers.

"There won't be a crowd here today," Driscoll told him. "Why don't you go to Shibe Park [where the Athletics were playing that day]?"

"I've been to Shibe Park," the vendor replied. "There's nobody there either."

LEE ALLEN

The trouble is, we are in a losing streak at the wrong time. If we were losing like this in the middle of the season, nobody would notice. But we are losing at the beginning of the season [1962, the Mets' first year], and this sets up the possibility of losing all 162 games.

CASEY STENGEL

Come out and see my Amazin' Mets. I been in the game a hundred years but I see new ways to lose I never knew existed before.

CASEY STENGEL

We was going to get you a birthday cake, but we figured you'd drop it.

CASEY STENGEL, to Marv Throneberry

———————

On his final at bat in the majors, Mets' catcher Joe Pignatano hit into a triple play in a game against the Cubs at Wrigley Field on the last day of the 1962 season.

RICH MARAZZI

———————

A lot of successful teams take their first step down when they become satisfied with their success rather than constantly moving forward. When they forget how they got to the top they lose what it takes to stay there.

CRAIG R. WRIGHT

I tell you what: I'm going to put in a pinch hitter for you because I don't want you to tie the record.

CONNIE MACK, after Eddie Joost had been struck out three times by Bob Feller

[Babe Ruth] and I are alike in only one way. We're both hard losers.

TY COBB

When all is said and done, all I want anyone to say of me is, "Earl Weaver—he sure was a good sore loser."

EARL WEAVER

With Bob Gibson, it wasn't that he wanted to win so much as that he didn't want to lose. He hated to lose. He just couldn't accept it.

TIM MCCARVER

The nice guys are all over there [in the Giants dugout]. In last place.

LEO DUROCHER

You don't have to be a rowdy to win pennants and you don't have to argue with umpires to win ball games.

We won pennants (more pennants than Brooklyn has ever won and in a tougher league, too) and every one of my players was a gentleman.

CONNIE MACK

The sun don't shine on the same dog's ass all the time.

CATFISH HUNTER, after losing to the Dodgers, 6–1, in the 1977 World Series.

4

Batting

Always have a belligerent, take-charge attitude up there. You have to cultivate quite a "mad on" while awaiting your turn at bat, a cold determination to ram the ball down the pitcher's throat. You'd be surprised how effective it is.

TY COBB

Keep your eye clear and hit 'em where they ain't.

WEE WILLIE KEELER

A good leadoff hitter is a pain in the ass to pitchers.

RICHIE ASHBURN

In all tools designed for men to swing there is a certain spot called the center of percussion. In a hammer it is in the head. In a baseball bat it is in the barrel, the exact location varying a little from bat to bat. A player knows he has hit the ball there when the bat follows through smoothly with no jar to arms or wrists.

MARSHALL SMELSER

I was playing in a game in St. Louis in 1917. [George] Sisler hit one along the ground. I run in and scoop it up. But I don't throw the ball. I hold it. There were ten perforations in it, one, two, three, four, ten perforations. I ran to the umpire and said he had better look at Sisler's bat. He had driven nails in it and filed them down.

BUCK WEAVER

Without probing, pseudopsychoanalytically, the satisfaction most humans seem to feel when they strike a ball solidly with a stick, the fun element in hitting is always evident.

LEONARD KOPPETT

[Wilcy Moore] had the perfect stance at the plate and the perfect swing. The only trouble was that he always swung in the same spot, no matter where the ball was, so that if he hit it, it was by accident. Ruth, after one look at him in batting practice at the training camp, bet him $300 to $100 that he wouldn't make three hits all season. He made five. When he got home he wrote the Babe a letter.

"The $300 come in handy," it said. "I used it to buy a fine pair of mules. I named one Babe and the other Ruth."

FRANK GRAHAM

Lefty [O'Doul] had a rope trick for overanxious young players who tended to lunge at the pitch. He would loop a rope around the kid's waist and stand back holding the loose end. If the kid lunged, the rope brought him up with a jerk.

RED SMITH

[Debs Garms] claims his success as a hitter is somewhat dependent on two bats which he uses. He throws the two bats in his back yard when he returns home in the fall, and when spring rolls around the several varieties of Texas winter weather have seasoned the bats until they are just right for hit production.

SPALDING-REACH OFFICIAL BASE BALL GUIDE, 1941

5

The Long Ball

and the Home Run Derby

. . . that rutting class of slugging batsmen who think of nothing else when they go to bat but that of gaining the applause of the "groundlings" by the novice's hit to the outfield of a "homer," one of the least difficult hits known to batting in baseball, as it needs only muscle and not brains to make it.

SPALDING BASEBALL GUIDE, 1886

I mean, it's unheard of for somebody to hit 70 home runs. I'm slightly in awe of myself.

MARK McGWIRE

It was a strange phenomenon when [Mark McGwire] walked to the plate. Everybody in the stands was anticipating a home run. It's hard to imagine anyone hitting a home run every time. At the same time, everyone knew the next homer could be the longest home run ever hit.

GARY GAETTI

Imagine, if you will, that the two players chasing Maris and Babe Ruth had been Albert Belle and Barry Bonds. People might still have paid attention—the way you pay attention to a car wreck.

STEVE ASCHBURNER

This summer (1977), a left-hand-swinging half-Chinese thirty-seven-year-old slugger named Sadaharu Oh struck the seven-hundred-and-fifty-sixth home run of his career, while playing for the Yomiuri Giants in Japan, and thus surpassed (in a way) Hank Aaron's lifetime mark; the qualifying parenthesis suggests that Japanese ballparks and Japanese pitchers are not all of major-league dimensions—a fact that the wonderful Oh admitted when he politely murmured, "I don't think I would do as well in American baseball."

ROGER ANGELL

This isn't life or death. We're like those surfer dudes out on the ocean. When you get up on a good wave, you ride it out as long as you can.

BARRY BONDS

I've always believed that the most important aspect of hitting is driving in runs. Runs batted in are more important than batting average, more important than home runs, more important than anything. That's what wins ball games: driving runs across the plate.

HANK GREENBERG

Give the batters credit. People have to realize that this is a golden age of hitting.

FRANK THOMAS

6

Base Running

Ducks on The Pond . . .

A defensive play is at least five times as hard to make as an offensive play. An error by a fielder can come from a bad throw, a bad hop of the ball, the muff of an easy chance, the ball hitting the runner or a mix-up in responsibility between shortstop and second baseman, or two outfielders, on a given play. But on offense, a man can run a play 100 times without variation or error. About the only mistake you can make is to stumble. Weighing those odds, I became extremely aggressive on the paths.

TY COBB

Sliding headfirst is the safest way to get to the next base, I think. And the fastest. You don't lose your momentum. . . . And there is one more important reason that I slide headfirst. It gets my picture in the newspaper.

PETE ROSE

Cheerful and popular, Rube Walker is a good receiver but his base running is a common subject of conversation.

"That guy," said a Dodger coach, "isn't as slow on the bases as he looks; he's slower."

JAMES T. FARRELL

He had larceny in his heart. But his feet were honest.

ARTHUR "BUGS" BAER, upon a failed stealing attempt by Ping Bodie

7

Pitching

I Used to Have A Rifle . . .

A man should always hold something in reserve, a surprise to spring when things get tight. If a pitcher has displayed his whole assortment to the batters in the early part of the game and has used all his speed and his fastest breaking curve, then, when the crisis comes, he "hasn't anything" to fall back on.

CHRISTY MATHEWSON

It's all part of the psychology of baseball. But the saddest words of all to a pitcher are three—"Take Him Out."

CHRISTY MATHEWSON

The real test comes when you are pitching with men on bases. Do not worry. Try to appear jolly and unconcerned. I have smiled often with the bases full with two strikes and three balls on the batter. This seems to unnerve.

RUBE FOSTER

Take four pitches—the fast ball, the curve, the slider and the screwball. Now throw these at different speeds, and you have twelve pitches. Next, throw each of these twelve pitches with a longarmed or shortarmed motion, and you have twenty-four pitches.

ED LOPAT

A curve ball may bother an ordinary hitter, but if a man is a really good hitter it's the old change of pace that causes him more trouble than all the freak deliveries in the world.

BABE RUTH

You have to remember that every good hitter is an egotist. If you can throw the fastball past them once, they'll make any adjustment to prevent it happening again. That makes the best of them gullible for a change-up.

WARREN SPAHN

Without the deception of the curve, baseball would have become just another sport for young men of premium size and strength.

MARTIN QUIGLEY

I am not positive whether a ball curves or not, but if this pitch does not curve, it would be well to notify a lot of baseball players who were forced to quit the game they love because of this pitch and may now be reached at numerous gas stations, river docks, and mental institutions.

EDDIE SAWYER

I don't know who the fellow was who came up with the first curve ball . . . I don't know when or where. But whoever he was, when he did it he took all the joy out of baseball.

BURT SHOTTON

. . . it's pretty hard to be lucky when your pitching is bad.

WALTER ALSTON

A mistake is a pitch I didn't execute well, one I left in an area where they could hit it. You don't call a ball a mistake because you miss the strike zone. That's not a mistake. A mistake, to me, is a ball I leave in the middle of the plate.

OREL HERSHISER

More and more, the starters in this league pitch backward—2–0 breaking balls and changeups, and 0–2 fastballs. They don't give in to you. It's a good way to pitch, if you can do it, because you can win that way.

PETE ROSE

The knuckleball looks particularly tempting if you are a lizard or a frog.

ROGER ANGELL

If a batter knows a pitcher will throw inside, he will be reluctant to dig in, and that's the edge the pitcher hoped he'd get.

TIM MCCARVER

I used to have a rifle,
I used to have a gun.
Lord, Lord,
I used to have a rifle,
I used to have a gun.
Now that ball floats over
Like a cinnamon bun.

BLUES SONG COMPOSED BY ROY BLOUNT, JR.

8

The Wet One

And Other Odd Deliveries . . .

I'd go to my mouth on every pitch. Not every pitch would be a spitball. Sometimes I'd go maybe two or three innings without throwing one. But I'd always have them looking for it.

Stanley Covaleski

I never tried to guess on [Grimes's] spitter. It broke just one way—in toward my head.

FRANK FRISCH

I used to chew slippery elm—the bark, right off the tree. Come spring the bark would get nice and loose and you could slice it free without any trouble. What I chewed was the fiber from inside, and that's what I put on the ball. That's what they called the foreign substance. The ball would break like hell, away from right-handed hitters, and in on lefties.

BURLEIGH GRIMES

I sometimes missed that sinker of [Johnny Allen's] day by a foot. It wasn't a curve and it wasn't a fastball, so I took it for granted it was a slider. But come to think of it, I did not in those days miss sliders by a foot.

JOE DIMAGGIO

The batter's sitting in the circle with a pine tar cloth. Puts tar on his hands, up to his elbows, if he wants, and rubs that bat and gets up there and squeezes and it sounds like a dad-gum car comin' by you, screechin' its wheels.

But if it's a poor old pitcher, he better not put his hand in his pocket, or touch his hat ever, 'cause they're gonna come runnin' to shake him down. I don't get it.

PREACHER ROE

Give the pitchers the right to apply saliva to the ball and you might give them the impression that they would be winked at if they again laved the ball with tobacco juice, annointed it with oils, powdered it with talcum, or even stuck phonograph needles in it.

BRANCH RICKEY

I see no need to revive it. All of us in baseball know that it's being thrown occasionally anyway.

WALTER ALSTON

———•••••———

Heed the cries of the hurlers in their desert of dire need by letting them use the spitter.

BILLY EVANS

———•••••———

Let them revive the spitter and help the pitchers make a living.

CASEY STENGEL

9

Catching

The Man in The Iron Mask . . .

I think we should look at the other end of the battery and consider the possibility that, year in and year out, each of the well-established veteran catchers is almost surely the most valuable player on his club . . .

ROGER ANGELL

A catcher and his body are like the outlaw and his horse. He's got to ride that nag till it drops.

JOHNNY BENCH

———•◦•◦•———

It's hard on you physically behind the plate. All that bending and kneeling. One way to help yourself is to get down to first base on [an infield bouncer] and do it every single time. You let yourself out a little, so you're not cramped up all day.

TOM HALLER

———•◦•◦•———

Masochists are what they are. A man has to love to get banged up if he deliberately chooses to be a catcher.

JIM BROSNAN

What I've seen over the past fifteen to twenty years is that the quickest route to the major leagues is by being a catcher.

RAY HAYWORTH

When I was making the transition from shortstop to catcher, one of the things they used to teach in that situation was to look the runner back to third before you threw to second. Well, if I've looked down there a thousand times, I still haven't seen anything. I look, all right, but as far as seeing if he's got a twenty-foot lead or a ten-foot lead or if he's standing on the bag, I would never see it because if you look long enough to actually see what's there, there's no way you're going to throw the man out at second.

BOBBY BRAGAN

Very few things happen on a major league baseball diamond by chance. Every pitch, every swing of the bat, every throw, is made with specific intention. And at the center of everything that happens is the catcher.

RON LUCIANO

I got one that can throw, but can't catch, and one that can catch but can't throw. And one who can hit but can't do either.

CASEY STENGEL

Anyway, who knows what the right pitch should have been? Most of the time you do everything right and a Mark McGwire, Tino Martinez or Barry Bonds will still pop it.

TIM McCARVER

10

Defense

Playing the Field . . .

Championship baseball teams are not founded on bats. They're built on a backbone of catching, pitching, a second-base combination and a center fielder.

CARL MAYS

———

. . . a fielder does not have to outguess a moving baseball; he has to anticipate which way it is likely to move before it starts.

LEONARD KOPPETT

Now that I think of it, some of the best preparation for outfield might be playing infield.

DICK HOWSER

I think the most difficult job in baseball is late-inning defense. It's like handling your homework in high school. You don't get any credit for just handling it because you're expected to do it, but if you don't do it you get docked.

TIM MCCARVER

The third base is not quite as important a position as the others, but it nevertheless requires its occupant to be a good player, as some very pretty play is frequently shown on this base.

SEYMOUR R. CHURCH (1902)

The shortstop—I don't know what's the hardest play for him. They're all hard, I guess. There's not much of a problem for him on the double play, because the whole situation's right in front of him, but the second baseman—he knows he's got to turn that thing, and the guy's breathing down his neck. You can get your legs torn up. More often than not, you see the second baseman turn it when he doesn't have a chance, really. The judgment of infielders is something.

CLETE BOYER

———◆———

Until Ozzie Smith began earning a salary with two commas in the numbers—$2 million—defense was not well remunerated. To paraphrase Ralph Kiner's celebrated aphorism, defense is not where the Cadillacs are. (Today Kiner would say Mercedes. Much has changed in America since the late 1940s.)

GEORGE F. WILL

You don't see too many big-legged second basemen, or big-legged shortstops. Why? Any scout could tell you. Range! The ones with range have tiny little legs.

GEORGE KISSELL

On September 13, 1942, Cub shortstop Len Merullo booted four plays in one inning. That morning his wife had given birth to a son. A sportswriter named the boy Boots Merullo.

JIM KAPLAN

The thing about the pickoff play is not just the twenty-six or twenty-seven guys you get a year—and I don't want to minimize that—but it just kills a ballclub. It happens to us every once in a while, and you can just feel the whole club go flat.

RAY MILLER

Take Lary Bowa and Garry Templeton in 1978. That year Bowa won his last Gold Glove, making only ten errors and leading the league in fielding percentage at .986. Templeton was an erratic twenty-two-year-old short-stop who led the league in errors and fielded only .953. What do we learn from this thirty-three-point differ-ence? Did we learn that Templeton—years away from his later knee trouble—showed spectacular range and fielded 82 more balls cleanly than Bowa did, despite playing one fewer game? Did we learn that Templeton led the league's shortstops in double plays with 108 compared with Bowa's 80?

CRAIG R. WRIGHT

———•••———

I don't like them fellas who drive in two runs and let in three.

CASEY STENGEL

[Bill Terry] concentrated entirely on defense. His theory was not to let the other club score and they'd beat themselves. Naturally most ball games are lost rather than won. Terry took it far beyond anything I ever knew—his entire approach in every game was defense. He didn't hit-and-run. He didn't go for the stolen base or any offensive plays at all. He just figured to score three or four runs.

PAUL RICHARDS

[Casey Stengel] relished double plays and was always looking for deft second basemen who could "make the pivot." He called the double play the most important play in baseball. "It's two-thirds of an inning!" he'd say. "One ground ball and [slap of the hands] two! You're out of the inning."

ROBERT W. CREAMER

11

Retirement

Learning to Be a Normal Person . . .

Having to leave the game is a very difficult adjustment to make, and that goes for every single ballplayer. Don't let any one of them tell you different.

BILL WAMBSGANSS

I don't miss the pitching but I can't say I don't miss the game. I miss it a little. There's a lot I don't want to get back to. . . . I think it's the life I miss—all the activities that's around baseball. I don't miss playing baseball but I miss . . . baseball. Baseball. Does that sound like a crazy man?

BOB GIBSON

. . . my years in baseball had their ups and downs, their strife and their torment. But the years I look at most fondly, and those I'd most like to live over, are the years when I was playing center field for the New York Giants.

FRED SNODGRASS

Getting out of baseball is usually a tough adjustment. It's really hard, excruciatingly so, for most guys. It didn't hit me that way, since I was happy to get out. The press gave me such a rough time I was looking forward to a quieter life. And now I'm having a great time.

ROGER MARIS

12

Managers

Peerless Leaders and Others . . .

"Don't give him anything good, but don't walk him."

ROGERS HORNSBY, to Burleigh Grimes

You can't stand alone against a new wave. It'll break you. That's why, when the Oakland ball club went to the long hair and moustaches, I went with them. When I managed the Red Sox, I had a butch haircut; with Oakland I was as hairy as the rest of them.

DICK WILLIAMS

There are three things the average man thinks he can do better than anyone else: build a fire, run a hotel and manage a baseball team.

ROCKY BRIDGES

What else are you gonna do when you get a second-division ball club? You've got a couple of young players on it, you work on them. Who else are you gonna work on? You keep after them. You ask them why they didn't make that throw. You ask them why they played that man there. Then for somebody else they turn out to be good ballplayers, but what of it? You helped to make them good ballplayers, didn't you?

CASEY STENGEL

Billy, what I can't understand is how I got so smart so fast, and you got so dumb.

> CASEY STENGEL, to Pittsburgh Manager Billy Meyer after the Pirates fell to sixth place in 1950 while Stengel's Yankees won the pennant and World Series

Two things happen to players on a championship team. First they think they're better than they are. Then when they begin to lose, they don't know what to do. That's when the manager has to step in and hold the wires. That's when the players depend on the manager more than the manager depends on the players.

> MILLER HUGGINS

There is no way 25 men, whose livelihoods depend on records compiled on the field, can be kept happy in a game that calls for only nine players.

> LEONARD KOPPETT

One day when I visited the Yankees bench I commented on the number of players Stengel was using nearly every day. Casey pointed to the row of pinstriped players who rode the bench with him. "None of those guys board here; they all work. That's why they give us twenty-five players—to let the manager play games with them."

FRED LIEB

Today big-league managers come and go. Charlie Finley hired and fired them, then George Steinbrenner outdid Finley. Led by Finley and followed by Steinbrenner, major-league owners have debased the lofty status of manager and stripped that position of much of the honor it once commanded.

RED BARBER

Good first base coaches, who can pitch and catch batting practice (though not exactly at the same time) and hit the highest fungoes in the league, are obviously a lot harder to find than managers.

MAURY ALLEN

I have never believed it effective to use ace against ace. From the grandstand and crowd point of view, this is all right, but when it comes to winning games throughout the season the percentage is against it. Why sacrifice an almost certain win for a possible low-score loss?

MICKEY COCHRANE

I think managing shortened my playing career, but I was a better manager when I was playing, when I could lead like a platoon sergeant in the field rather than as a general sitting back on his duff in a command post.

FRANK FRISCH

The crowd which cheers the players has little conception of the trials and tribulations of the manager who crouches unseen and forgotten . . . in the corner of the bench. The public does not realize that he is dealing with twenty-two ultra-independent athletes, vulgarly healthy, frankly outspoken, and unawed by any authority or pomp. Only persons who have one child, which possesses four grandparents, and twenty or thirty aunts all trying to spoil it, can understand in full the difficulties of the manager's job.

JOHNNY EVERS

I had another system I used now and then when I wanted to know who was staying out late. It was very simple. I gave the night elevator operator a brand new baseball and told him to get the players to autograph it for him. So as they came in at night, they'd sign the ball. The next day he'd show me the ball and tell me what time each man came in.

EDDIE SAWYER

13

Men in Blue

If That's You, Leo, He's Out . . .

Outside of the nine players on each side there is another important personage, known as "The Umpire." He is not placed there as a target for the malediction of disappointed spectators. He is of flesh and blood, and has feelings just the same as any other human being.

JOHN MONTGOMERY WARD (1888)

———

Baseball is the only sport that lets the managers and coaches go out onto the field and rant and rave.

DURWOOD MERRILL

One thing there is that affords a baseball umpire consolation, and that is the thought that he can die only once, and then never more.

THE SPORTING NEWS, 1888

There are no close plays. A man is always out or safe, or it is a ball or a strike, and the umpire, if he is a good man and knows his business, is always right. For instance, I am always right.

SILK O'LOUGHLIN

When Lord Bill [Byron] called what McGraw thought was a bad one, Mac would start for the umpire, and Byron would begin to sing, "Here Comes McGraw" to the tune of Mendelssohn's "Wedding March."

JOE WILLIAMS

Johnson was working against us and they was two out and Collins on second base and Silk [O'Loughlin] called a third strike on Gandil that was down by his corns. So Gleason hollered "All right Silk you won't have to go to war. You couldn't pass the eye test." So Silk told him to get off the field. So then I hollered something at Silk and he hollered back at me "That will be all from you you big busher." So I said "You are a busher yourself you busher." So he said:

"Get off the bench and let one of the ball players sit down."

RING LARDNER

The evidence on which players are punished is strictly ex parte, for the man sentenced is never heard in his own behalf. The umpire is judge, jury, and prosecuting attorney and is well termed "the autocrat of the diamond."

CHICAGO NEWS, June 23, 1908

February 22, 1889. — Umpire Magill, with a bat, fractured the skull of a spectator who took exception to his rulings in an exhibition game. Chattanooga.

SEYMOUR R. CHURCH (1902)

It's eider dis or dat wid me. Dere ain't no in-between.

BILL GUTHRIE, upon being asked how close a called ball came to being a strike

If dat bat comes down, you're outta da game.

BILL GUTHRIE, after a batter heaved his bat skyward upon being called out on strikes

The greatest umpire who ever lived was Bill Klem. He summed up his profession in one terse sentence: "Umpire the ball."

RED BARBER

14

Scouting

Beating around the Bushes . . .

Scouts are still probably the lowest paid employees in the baseball chain.

MAURY ALLEN

———•·••·•———

The draft has more or less made every club equal, and maybe it's made baseball better, but I think it's changed scouting for the worse.

HOWIE HAAK

. . . the writer, Harold Parrott, told an interesting one about "Vinegar Bill" Essick, the Yankee scout who signed Joe Gordon. He was trying to sign a young prospect named Johnny Lindell. The night he called on Lindell's parents, Essick played a few selections from Brahms. And the parents hearing the scout at the piano, decided that after all, baseball couldn't be so rowdy. Johnny Lindell was signed, and his batting helped the New York Yankees to win a World Series.

JAMES T. FARRELL

The draft is socialistic. For one thing, it gives the teams with the poorest records the earliest selections in each round. It's part of a push to equalize talent from team to team—but there never has been equalization of talent in baseball, and there never will be.

PAUL OWENS

Listen, I'd take my chances any day on guys like [Dave] Parker instead of college kids. You start goin' after these college ballplayers and you go right down the drain. You pay good money, and then if they're not in the major leagues in two years they quit on you.

HOWIE HAAK

You can draft all the track runners you want, but if they don't hit, they're not going to play. If you can't swing the bat, it's going to be rough, real tough.

HEP CRONIN

The scout who deserves credit is the guy who discovers someone the others missed or underrated, like our guy in New Jersey who recommended Mark Lemke. We got him in the twenty-seventh round. Nobody else seemed to have him on his list, and yet he made it to the big leagues.

HEP CRONIN

If scouting were just a matter of signing the guys who hit the home runs and pitch the no-hitters, anybody could do it. But the major league prospect might be the guy who has something special even though he struck out swinging or overthrew the third baseman from right field or walked nine batters. Tools we call them: speed, arm strength, range, hands, bat speed.

BUCK O'NEIL

Looks like Tarzan. Runs like Jane.

SCOUTING REPORT

15

The Negro Leagues
and the End of the Color Line

Yet when you look back, what people didn't realize, and
still don't, was that we got the ball rolling on integration
in our whole society. Remember, this was before Brown
versus the Board of Education of Topeka. When Branch
Rickey signed Jackie, Martin Luther King was a student
at Morris College. We showed the way it had to be done,
by just keeping on and being the best we could.

BUCK O'NEIL

We suggest that every citation for a record set before 1950 should bear an asterisk, with the following explanation: * Set before the American and National Leagues became the major leagues.

JOHN B. HOLWAY

If you want to know the truth, Judy, there are just too many of you to go in.

CONNIE MACK, when asked by Judy Johnson why as a star black player he did not make the major leagues

I made more money when I was in the majors, and the caliber of baseball and the playing conditions were better, but I had more fun with the Negro leagues.

MONTE IRVIN

At the time when I was playing [in the Negro leagues], most of the owners were in the numbers business, because that was the only way a black man could garner enough money to field a team.

MONTE IRVIN

The three greatest men in Negro baseball were [Cum] Posey, [J. L.] Wilkinson, and Abe Saperstein of Birmingham.

TED RADCLIFFE, on the promoters of black baseball

The raw talent of the players [in the two Negro leagues] was generally major-league caliber, but in other ways, the leagues were not at that level. The owners had a loosely formed league and they stayed together, but they were not very well organized.

MONTE IRVIN

Whether we get any recognition for it may be considered beside the point. We want Jackie [Robinson] to have a chance.

J. L. WILKINSON

The real meaning of the Jackie Robinson Revolution was not to get black players into major league baseball ... The real meaning of the revolution was to get black owners out.

JOHN B. HOLWAY

The Brooklyn Dodgers today purchased the contract of Jackie Roosevelt Robinson from the Montreal Royals. He will report immediately.

BRANCH RICKEY, news release issued April 10, 1947

When [Hank] Thompson and I reported to the Polo Grounds, our uniforms were laid out for us. I went over to the locker to get dressed, and when I put on the New York Giants uniform for the first time, that had to be one of the greatest thrills of my life. It was like a dream coming true, and something that I never expected to ever happen. I thought about the long road that I had traveled to get there, and the fact that it was finally happening was a feeling that is indescribable.

MONTE IRVIN

When Jackie Robinson died in 1972 of diabetes and hypertension, some wrote that his coming was no big thing and would have happened sooner or later. Others, more cynical, described Rickey's driving force as greed. But the fact is that before Branch Rickey no one had done it or even seriously proposed doing it. And that is his legacy.

MURRAY POLNER

Did you ever notice that the teams that signed more black players faster tended to win more games?

WILLIE MAYS

16

The World Series

It is safe to say that no cynic has ever played in a World Series.

———•••••———

Casey [Stengel] always had something to say, even in those days. I remember, just before the first game (of the 1916 Series), during batting practice, Duffy Lewis and I were walking across the outfield and as we passed him Casey said, "Hello, boys. What do you think your losing share is going to come to?"

ERNIE SHORE

It's like the Fourth of July, New Year's Eve, and your birthday all wrapped in one.

TOM SEAVER

———•••———

I had talked to [Ernie White's] wife before the game and I asked her if she kept score when Ernie pitched. She said, "I try. I start out keeping score, but if he stays in there for a few innings I chew up my pencil and I haven't got anything left to write with." I saw her after the [1942 World Series] game in the Stadium—White pitched a 2–0 shutout—and she smiled and said, "I chewed up four pencils today."

RED BARBER

———•••———

It doesn't get any better than winning the World Series.

CHUCK KNOBLAUCH

17

Patrons of the Game

American Sportsmen in Action . . .

So, too, the crowd as a whole plays the role of Greek chorus to the actors on the field below. It reflects every action, every movement, every changing phase of the game. It keens. It rejoices. It moans. It applauds and gives great swelling murmurs of surprise and appreciation, or finds relief in huge, Gargantuan laughs. I can stand outside of a ball park and listen to the crowd and come close to telling exactly what is happening on the diamond inside.

PAUL GALLICO

The voice of the republic is not a pontifical blessing from a high window or the cry of an imperial herald in a palace court. It is the voice of a crowd, best heard in its spontaneity in a ball park.

MARSHALL SMELSER

The lesser wonders of baseball—the sacrifice fly, the three-six-three double play, the wrong-side hit-and-run bouncer through a vacated infield sector, the right-field-to-third-base peg that cuts down a lead runner, the extended turn at bat against an obdurate pitcher that ends with a crucial single squiggled down the middle—are most appreciated by the experienced fan, who may in time also come to understand that expertise is the best defense against partisanship.

ROGER ANGELL

The feebleness of the home team's play . . . caused much dissatisfaction, which was rather warmly expressed.

BALTIMORE SUN, 1874

———◆◆◆———

Whoever has not experienced the pleasure of taking a young lady to her first game of ball should seize the first opportunity to do so. Her remarks about plays, her opinions of different players and the umpire, and the questions she will ask concerning the game, are all too funny to be missed. She is a violent partisan and at once takes strong sides, and if her favorite team fails to bat well she characterizes the opposing pitcher as a "horrid creature"; or when the teams have finished practicing she wants to know, with charming ingenuousness, "which won."

JOHN MONTGOMERY WARD (1888)

It has been decided that the American baseball fan should have a distinctive dress. A choice has been made from among the more popular styles and the following has been designated as regulation, embodying, as it does, the spirit and tone of the great national pastime.

Straw hat, worn well back on the head; one cigar, unlighted, held between teeth; vest worn but unbuttoned and open, displaying both a belt and suspenders, with gold watchchain connecting the bottom pockets.

ROBERT BENCHLEY (1922)

———

There are more good batters and umpires and all-round ball players in the grand stand within one's hearing, than are to be found in both the contesting teams.

JOHN MONTGOMERY WARD (1888)

Today only among the bleacher regulars can we find the fan who resembles the typical fan of 1901–1917. These earlier and narrower fans knew the differing styles of their heroes in the way that an art critic knows brushwork, or a music critic can recognize a brass section.

MARSHALL SMELSER

Thirty years ago the applauding of an opposing team was looked upon as little less than treason. It is very common now for the stands to give the opposing team, even an individual player, an ovation.

JOHN MCGRAW

A people who can become as excited about anything as the majority of New Yorkers can about the baseball pennant is far from being lost to hope.

NEW YORK AMERICAN, Oct. 9, 1908

Our greatest chance, I believe, lies in the fact that we will finish the season at home. The encouragement of a friendly big city is no small factor in a team's success.

CHRISTY MATHEWSON, Aug. 9, 1908

After the game a cushion battle between 3,000 in the stands and 5,000 in the field raged for fifteen minutes, during which many women were injured and their hats demolished. The police were powerless. In this way the crowd expressed its joy over the victory.

NEW YORK WORLD, Aug. 30, 1908

Well, throwing things on the field is not my idea of a well-rounded human being.

STEVE GARVEY, when asked by a reporter what he thought of the fans at Yankee Stadium

This year, after a game with the Orioles—which the Yankees won—I waited outside the players' gate with Elrod Hendricks, the Orioles' coach who once played for the Yankees. A howling mob stood behind police barricades, jeering and screaming obscenities at each of the Oriole players who boarded a waiting team bus. This was standard, Hendricks assured me—for Yankee Stadium.

DAVID FALKNER

Over in Brooklyn they don't bet that the home team will win—they make book on how much the opposing forces will win by. This sport furnishes the only uncertainty of the entertainment.

W. H. AULICK, *New York Times*, May 31, 1908

The bottle has a peculiar significance in Brooklyn. Were there a baseball crest for the Dodgers it would show a pop bottle rampant on a field strewn with umpires.

JOE WILLIAMS

They came to root, and they never gave up. It was Brooklyn against the world. They were not only complete fanatics, but they knew baseball like the fans of no other city. It was exciting to play there. It was a treat.

LEO DUROCHER

Jeez! It's Poil Harbor for da Giants.

BROOKLYN DODGER FAN, quoted after Leo Durocher was appointed manager of the New York Giants, replacing Mel Ott

"Poison" is Brooklynese for person. A fan in Ebbets Field is supposed to have complained, "Every time you look up those Waner boys are on base. It's always the little poison on third and the big poison on foist."

RED SMITH

————•••••————

If I close my eyes against the sun [at Fenway Park], all at once I am back at Ebbets Field, a young girl once more in the presence of my father, watching the players of my youth on the grassy field below. There is magic in this moment, for when I open my eyes and see my sons in the place where my father once sat, I feel an invisible bond between our three generations, an anchor of loyalty linking my sons to the grandfather whose face they never saw but whose person they have already come to know through the most timeless of all sports, the game of baseball.

DORIS KEARNS GOODWIN

I enjoy Shea Stadium. But the fans are something else. I look upon each game there as an experience. I get to go to a zoo and don't have to pay admission.

PETE ROSE

———————

I never mingled with people in Philadelphia. I developed a bad taste for the city because of the fans. They cheered when you did well, but when they got mean, they were meaner than anyone else. They booed Gus [Zernial] when he was being carried off the field with a broken shoulder—and he was our most popular player! They used to throw beer and mustard at the players' wives from the upper deck. My wife almost had a nervous breakdown because of that.

The real article is the man who knows most of the players by sight, as they appear on the field, but wouldn't know more than one or two of them if he saw them on the street, struggles hard to keep an accurate score and makes a mistake on every other play, or doesn't attempt to score at all, disputes every statement made by his neighbors in the bleachers whether he knows anything about said statement or not, heaps imprecations on the umpire and the manager, thinks something is a bonehead play when it really is good, clever baseball, talks fluently about Mathewson's "inshoot," believes that Hank O'Day has it in for the home team and is purposely making bad decisions, and says "Branfield is going to bat for Moore" when Walsh is sent in to hit for Chalmers.

RING LARDNER

On the way out, in the eighth inning, I saw a young groupie approach George Foster just outside the Cincinnati clubhouse. "Sign my pants!" she said to him. "Please, George, sign my pants!"

We both looked, and, sure enough, her bluejeans were heavily autographed.

"I don't sign clothing," Foster said.

ROGER ANGELL

18

The Hall of Fame

This Hall of Fame thing is bigger than anything I ever saw.

CASEY STENGEL

———•••———

Records, yes I've got a few of those too, but records are made to be broken. If you've got one that stands up, well you know that somebody might come along and break it. And then they might not, that's what baseball records are all about. But the Hall of Fame, that will be there forever.

HOYT WILHELM

You look at the lineup we put on the field for the first game of that [1932] World Series and you'll see we had six fellows in there who are in the Hall of Fame today—Ruth, Gehrig, Combs, Dickey, Red Ruffing, and myself.

JOE SEWELL

I know it's hard to get into the Hall of Fame. I don't know what kept me out—maybe it was the writers—but I finally made it and I thank God for it. I didn't know I'd ever feel like this.

BILL TERRY

Quite a few come up to be inducted and never come back. Ted Williams is one. He's a fellow who should be a leader in this regard, and isn't. People should be able to see these players without charge. I've always offered to go any place for this sort of thing, and I've gone to a few places.

BILL TERRY

The only thing I ever wanted to do was to put one foot into the major leagues, but they didn't want it. Now I can thank each and every veteran on the [Hall of Fame] committee for allowing me to smell the roses . . . I love baseball, and today it looks like baseball loves me.

RAY DANDRIDGE, at Cooperstown, 1988

He came in the front door [of the Hall of Fame], but the original plan was for him to go in the back door: into a special wing for Negro-leaguers. A lot of people, black and white, were angry when that plan was announced, and I think Satchel shook them up when he said, "The only change is that baseball has turned Satchel from a second-class citizen into a second-class immortal." The outcry was such that Commissioner Bowie Kuhn reversed the decision and put Satchel in the same room with Ruth and Mathewson and Jackie Robinson.

BUCK O'NEIL

We never thought we'd get in the Hall of Fame. It was so far from us, we didn't even consider it. We didn't even think it would some day come to reality. We thought the way we were playing was the way it was going to continue. I never had any dream it would come. But last night I felt like I was part of it at last.

BUCK LEONARD

19

Continuity and Innovation

Though Much Is Taken, Much Abides . . .

In the country of baseball days are always the same.

DONALD HALL

———•×•———

Baseball's essential rules for place and for play were established, to my reckoning, with almost no exceptions of consequence, by 1895.

A. BARTLETT GIAMATTI

The coincidence . . . of electronic public-address systems and World War II brought about the current practice of playing the anthem before every baseball game (and, by extension, before practically every major sports event). It is estimated that a twenty-year veteran like Willie Mays heard "The Star-Spangled Banner" played 3000 times. Usually badly.

ROBERT W. CREAMER

But the truth of the matter, of course, is that baseball has hardly changed at all. The game on the field, though played now by young millionaires and watched, idly and imperfectly, by millions of us in our living rooms, is almost exactly the same game that we learned as children, and that our fathers and grandfathers watched when they were children.

ROGER ANGELL

It is the same game that Moonlight Graham played in 1905. It is a living part of history, like calico dresses, stone crockery, and threshing crews eating at outdoor tables. It continually reminds us of what it once was, like an Indian-head penny in a handful of new coins.

W. P. KINSELLA

The day Custer lost at the Little Bighorn, the Chicago White Sox beat the Cincinnati Red Legs, 3–2. Both teams wore knickers. And they're still wearin' them today.

CHARLES O. FINLEY

As we look at change in baseball, we see that one unchanging feature is the way its professional players have exploited, mitigated, and circumvented changes in rules in order to succeed, or just to survive, in merciless competition.

MARTIN QUIGLEY

The baseball mania has run its course. It has no future as a professional endeavor.

CINCINNATI GAZETTE, 1870

[Night baseball]'s just a fad. It'll never last after the novelty wears off.

ED BARROW

Night baseball again was fairly well attended, and will continue to be until its novelty wears off.

SPALDING'S OFFICIAL BASEBALL GUIDE (1938)

The DH is a tenth player. Softball is ten players, baseball is nine.

DWIGHT GOODEN

Of course, it's much harder to deaden the ball on Astro-Turf than it is on grass. I think a lot of managers feel that the AstroTurf is to the advantage of the hitters, and I think they turn them loose a little more than they used to.

WALTER ALSTON

On turf the ball comes to me and says, "Catch me." On grass it says, "Look out, sucker."

GREG PRYOR

The infield game was something else. Nothing normal about it. There were easy two-hop plays, and occasionally a ball might bounce three times in the infield, on a deep play, before it was handled. There were few good plays by traditional standards.

EUGENE J. MCCARTHY

If a horse can't eat it, I don't want to play on it.

DICK ALLEN

I do not like artificial turf. I like the game that artificial turf creates.

BILL JAMES

I don't know. I never smoked artificial turf.

DOUG RADER, upon being asked about the difference between grass and artificial turf. (But see page ix. Also attributed to Tug McGraw.)

20

Problems

Beanballs, Black Sox, Drugs, etc. . . .

From its earliest days, baseball has indulged gamblers, fixers, drunkards, brawlers, disreputable moguls, bad actors, felons, homicidal maniacs, crooked umpires, vindictive owners, pyromaniacal fans, and at least one ax murderer.

STEPHEN S. HALL

The beanball is one of the meanest things on earth, and no decent fellow would use it. The beanball pitcher is a potential murderer. If I were a batter and thought that the pitcher really tried to bean me, I'd be inclined to wait for him outside the park with a baseball bat.

WALTER JOHNSON

Of all the ongoing scandals in baseball, the worst by far is the beanball. Its perpetrators have several excuses for condoning the crime. "It's part of the game," they say. Or, "I got to have the inside of the plate." Or, "I was just trying to move him back."

It used to be "part of the game" to call all Jewish players Moe. It used to be part of the game to have no black players. It used to be part of the game for players to wear no protective headgear or catcher's gear. Baseball discarded these idiocies, but not the beanball.

JIM KAPLAN

I had the reputation of being the kind of pitcher who'd knock you down if you got a hit off me, but I wouldn't always do it on the first pitch. Maybe I'd throw you a knuckleball instead. Then a curveball. Then a nice change of pace. You'd start to think, Good, he forgot about that hit, and right then—whap—down you'd go. [Laughs delightedly.]

LEON DAY

[Eddie Collins] seemed to have no sympathy for any of [the Black Sox], not even Jackson who was practically an illiterate, or young Buck Weaver who had been caught up in the polluted swirl of bad company, nor did he have any patience with the explanation that a penurious owner had shabbily underpaid hired hands.

"They were old enough to know the difference between right and wrong," he would say with cold level finality.

JOE WILLIAMS

It was like hearing that my church had sold out.

BABE RUTH, on the Black Sox scandal

———●•◦•●———

The extent of the involvement [of major league players in drugs] became pathetically clear when Montreal outfielder Tim Raines, the National League's leading base stealer, admitted that he often dove headfirst into second base during a steal so as to protect the gram bottle of cocaine he kept in his back pocket.

STEPHEN S. HALL

21

Owners and Administrators

The Bucks Stop Here . . .

The greatest evil with which the business has of recent years to contend is the unscrupulous methods of some of its "managers." Knowing no such thing as professional honor, these men are ever ready to benefit themselves, regardless of the cost to an associate club. The reserve rule itself is a usurpation of the players' rights, but it is, perhaps, made necessary by the peculiar nature of the base-ball business, and the player is indirectly compensated by the improved standing of the game.

JOHN MONTGOMERY WARD (1888)

The reserve clause exists for two reasons. One, to cut down on the money the ballplayers get, and two, to give a feeling of power to men who like to play God over other people's lives.

CURT FLOOD

Baseball—like our movies, like our newspapers and magazines—has fallen into the hands of rich, vulgar people who neither love nor understand it.

HAL CROWTHER

The players had no say. If you talked about a union it was like being a Communist, so nobody talked about unions or other players' contracts. There were in-equities—the general managers battered down the players.

RUBE WALKER

I found out a long time ago that there is no charity in baseball, and that every owner must make his own fight for existence.

JACOB RUPPERT

The other clubs would do better to stop worrying about breaking up the Yankees and start worrying about catching up to the Yankees!

JACOB RUPPERT

Mr. Breadon, if you ever threw $2,000 out the window, your arm would still be holding onto it.

JOE MEDWICK, to Sam Breadon at contract time

The very first thing I did when I came into Brooklyn in late 1942 was to investigate the approval of ownership for a Negro player. There was a timeliness about the notion. The Negro in America was legally but never morally free. I thought: if the right man with control of himself could be found . . .

BRANCH RICKEY

There was something about [Branch Rickey] of the travelling medicine-show man, something of W. C. Fields. But his ultimate alteration of the game, the destruction of baseball's color bar, was an act of national significance—an essential remedy that had awaited a man of subtlety and stubborn moral courage to bring it about.

ROGER ANGELL

I couldn't tell Rickey to get better players because he was too pompous to allow us to talk to him about such matters.

RALPH KINER

In the nineteen-fifties and early sixties, when some old baseball franchises—the Dodgers, the Giants, the Athletics, the Senators, and the rest—were first ripped loose from their traditional cities and their fanatically loyal lifetime fans, and after that, when handfuls of new and vapid teams were invented, the fans saw, many of them for the first time, that the owners were in this game, first and always, for the money.

ROGER ANGELL

Many baseball writers took him for a warm friend, without recognizing that, as with an underboiled potato, [Walter] O'Malley's warmth was mostly external.

ROGER KAHN

George [Steinbrenner] can't see that. Like I said, when he signs someone for big money, all of a sudden they become his bosom buddies, but the players who have been around for a year or two, he just thinks, Goddamn, they should be happy he's building the club, adding players to make the Yankees win again, that he's doing this for me, for Willie [Randolph], for whoever. But it isn't that way. No one wants to feel that he's being underpaid, I don't give a damn who you are, whether you're a truck driver, a secretary, or the president of General Motors.

SPARKY LYLE

It's a baseball fan's birthright to maintain a lifelong ambivalence toward the Yankees, respecting their great players while condemning an ownership that pays cash for its Ruths and Jacksons, brazenly buys players for every stretch, and regularly cashiers lovable old managers like Stengel and Lemon.

THOMAS BOSWELL

[Marge] Schott and Steinbrenner are so disgusting the other owners had to pretend to punish them to keep the press and politicians at bay. They get the headlines. But don't overlook lower-profile swine like Jerry Reinsdorf of the Chicago White Sox, who methodically harassed and humiliated Carlton Fisk, the last of the old-time work-ethic ballplayers, and dumped him without apology at mid-season after 25 years in the game.

HAL CROWTHER

In 1981, when George Steinbrenner was berating his Yankees after a loss in the playoffs against Milwaukee, one voice broke the silence with a brief rebuttal. "Go screw yourself, George." Catcher Rick Cerone, naturally.

THOMAS BOSWELL

I've worked for Charlie [Finley] and I've worked for George Steinbrenner and I've survived to tell about it. Not many others can make that statement.

EDDIE LOPAT

———•••———

Moneygrubbers? Not really. Sportsmen? Hardly. Perhaps the most suitable description is the most direct one: owners. They own.

And they don't like you to forget it.

LEONARD KOPPETT

22

Commissioners

From Landis to Selig . . .

I think [Kenesaw Mountain Landis] was totally honest, but he was vain, egotistical, dominating, and a show-off. He swore like a trooper, chewed tobacco, and was fond of bourbon whiskey.

FRED LIEB

———————

If a black boy can make it on Okinawa and Guadalcanal, hell, he can make it in baseball.

A. B. (HAPPY) CHANDLER

The years I was commissioner there were three or four writers, some of them old friends, who were never in my office and never called me up. It seemed that they did go out of their way to be critical. I don't know, maybe it was their style of writing. Commissioner Chandler was heavily criticized, too. So was Mr. Eckert. That's part of the job. But any man who says he doesn't pay attention to criticism is crazy. In your heart there is a scar.

FORD C. FRICK

By the end of [Peter V.] Ueberroth's rookie year as commissioner [1985], there was evidence that his charm did not give him seven-league boots. He was learning the bitter lesson that his baseball post was more a sticky morass than a stepping stone to high political office.

DAVID QUENTIN VOIGT

Owners have a duty to take into consideration that they own a part of America's national pastime in trust. This trust sometimes requires putting self-interest second.

FAY VINCENT

Bud Selig has a mandate and an opportunity. He had all these years of this nebulous, let's-build-concensus garbage, and now he has a strong base. Wouldn't it be wonderful if he turned around and listened to no man?

He loves history. Suppose, over the next five years of his term, he made every decision in the best interest of baseball and built on this. If he said, "This must stop" and "We have to do this" and "Television, we have to take control of our own destiny."

It might be a one-term shot but what a legend he could leave at this time.

MIKE VEECK

23

Baseball Wives

Family Considerations . . .

Women are never no help around the ball club. Wives don't do no good.

ROGERS HORNSBY

—•◦•—

As a rule I do not approve a wife's accompanying her husband on the road trips. She seems to distract his attention.

JOHN MCGRAW

You can't even make love to your husband when you want to. You have to wait for an off day.

CYNDY (FORMERLY MRS. STEVE) GARVEY

—●·●·●—

I don't know anything about baseball. That was Dizzy's business. But I do know how the money is to be got and what to do with it. When one member of the firm is lacking in practical sense it's a good thing the other member has it, and that's where I come in.

PATRICIA DEAN

—●·●·●—

Mrs. [Laraine] Durocher was listening to my broadcast of a Brooklyn game. She got the word about Leo's new job with the Giants. Without hesitation she snapped off the radio with the remark, "What am I listening to this for?"

RED BARBER

That old Dodger club was very close. Most of us had been together for a number of years, and when we'd gather in the clubhouse that first day of spring training, it was like when you were a kid going back to school in the fall with all your school friends. We could hardly wait.

Our wives once in a while got a little jealous because we spent so much time together. Lots of times after a road game, ten or fifteen of us would go out and spend the evenings together.

DUKE SNIDER

———

When I first got to know Satchel Paige, he had a wife whose nickname was Toad. She was a barmaid at the Grand Hotel in Chicago, and when we played the Chicago American Giants, we would go there after the game. We'd say, "Hey, Toad! Where's Satchel?" "You asking me where Satchel is?" she'd say. "I should be asking you. I haven't seen him in weeks. If you see him, tell him to give me a call."

MONTE IRVIN

All year at Three Rivers Stadium, the field loudspeakers blasted out the Pirates' theme song during the seventh-inning stretch—a thumping, catchy disco-rock number, "We Are Family," by the Sister Sledge group. This time, with the late-summer shadows deepening and the championship at last in hand, the wives of the Pittsburgh players suddenly moved forward from their seats, just behind the screen, and clambered up onto a low, curving shelf that rims the field behind home plate. At first, there were only a few of them, but more and more of the young women ran down the aisles and were pulled up onto the sudden stage, and then they were all dancing there together arm in arm, jiving and boogieing and high-kicking in rhythm, in their slacks and black-and-gold scarves and long, ballplayer-wives' fur coats, all waving and laughing and hugging and shaking their banners in time to the loud music.

ROGER ANGELL

I really think the baseball organization should pay more attention to the players' families when they come from a different country. It's not only the player that has to get along in this country. He comes with a wife and some-times kids. Some wives don't even come to the games because they don't even understand the language.

WALESKA (MRS. BERNIE] WILLIAMS

A ballplayer gets so used to everybody treating him well and looking after him that he begins to expect that at home. I was just telling Bernie today that he can't expect the same treatment at home that he gets out here at the ballpark.

WALESKA WILLIAMS

24

Sportswriters and Other Scribes

The View from the Press Box . . .

You could always tell a player's worth by the space given to his obit in the *Sporting News*, and Taylor [Spink] gave me the big ones. I covered the passing of the real greats, Nap Lajoie, Hans Wagner, Bobby Wallace, Walter Johnson, Paul Waner, Grover Cleveland Alexander, Mickey Cochrane, and dozens of others. I wrote so many of these "last rites" that Bob Broeg, the gifted baseball writer and sports editor of the *St. Louis Post-Dispatch*, dubbed me the "baseball undertaker."

FRED LIEB

When I entered the game we received only a few lines as news. These few lines expanded into columns and pages; in ratio the crowds in our ball parks grew and grew and grew. News, like advertising, is a powerful momentum behind any enterprise.

The professional sporting world was created and is being kept alive by the services extended by the press.

CONNIE MACK

One of the most famous paragraphs in baseball literature was the one the late John Lardner wrote: "Floyd Caves Herman never tripled into a triple play, but he once doubled into a double play, which is the next best thing."

JIM MURRAY

The Colts were beaten and rained upon, in that order, at Mooers Field yesterday.

> SHELLEY ROLFE (My all-time favorite lead sentence about a baseball game, written about the Richmond Colts of the old Piedmont League, in the *Richmond, Va., Times-Dispatch,* c. 1948)

Dave Kingman, Oakland's designated hitter, was slapped with a $3,000 fine by A's officials after he had a live rat delivered in a box to Susan Fornoff, baseball writer for the *Sacramento Bee*, in the Kansas City press box on June 23. A note attached to the rat's tail read: "My name is Susan."

> CLIFFORD KACHLINE

I'm always amazed at the amount of hostility among the male writers that is directed at the players. Obviously, not all the writers are failed athletes, but there are far too many of them.

> STEPHANIE SALTER

[Jim] Ogle was a Yankee fan and he reacted to players purely on how much they were helping the Yankees to win. Charm, personality, intelligence—nothing counted. Only winning. Ogle didn't even have the pretense of objectivity. He was the only writer in the press box who would take the seventh-inning stretch in the Yankee half.

JIM BOUTON

Writers don't fire managers. Losses fire managers. Writers, even the self-absorbed ones who think of themselves as poets, baseball gurus, or press box Woodwards and Bernsteins, don't make a team lose. They might make teams miserable or uptight, but they ultimately don't make teams lose.

PETER PASCARELLI

I've seen sports writers with World Series rings, and they wear them as though they had something to do with the winning of the World Series. Maybe they're entitled to them. Maybe their biased cheerfulness helped the club. I wouldn't know. I would not wear a World Series ring.

JIMMY CANNON

You tell [Charles] Dryden [of the *New York American*] that he is standing on the brink of an abscess and if he ain't careful, I'll push him in.

ANDREW FREEDMAN, owner of the New York Giants, 1895–1902

Ballplayers shouldn't gripe about reporters. A ballplayer should stay on a reporter's good side. Say nice things. Admire his clothes. Compliment him on his t-shirt.

ANDY VAN SLYKE

It was just before Opening Day and an earnest New York baseball writer asked, "Leo, do you intend to get your team off to a fast start this year?" Durocher looked at him contemptuously and rasped, "No, you stupid son of a bitch, I'm gonna lose the first ten games."

ROBERT W. CREAMER

After [Don Larsen's perfect game in the 1956 World Series], manager Casey Stengel was asked the dumbest question in the history of journalism: Was that the best game he had ever seen Larsen pitch? Stengel said: "So far."

GEORGE F. WILL

I can still hear Pete Rose, on the top of the dugout screaming, "Fuck you, Shakespeare."

JIM BOUTON, after publication of his book *Ball Four*

Jimmy [Cannon]'s spoken lines were as swift and pointed as the ones he wrote. At a World Series he was scolding about Baltimore fans—he was capable of throwing a hate on a whole city—and a press box companion demurred: "Oh, Jimmy, people are alike everywhere." "Like Francis of Assisi and Adolf Eichmann?" he shot back.

RED SMITH

As a writer, Dan [Daniel] did not subscribe to the Hemingway school that prefers the simple "he said" to "he declared" or "replied" or "remonstrated" or "cried" or "growled," etc. Dan coined his own verbs: "he exuberated," or "he vehemed." . . . Sometimes when he was holding forth on some subject his friend Frank Graham would say, "Oh, Dan, stop veheming."

RED SMITH

I was talking to this sports writer who said to me, "Why aren't the ball players as colorful as they used to be?" "I don't know," I told him. "Now let me ask you one. Why aren't the sports writers as colorful as they used to be?"

LEFTY GOMEZ

Tom Swope, the old Cincinnati baseball writer who died recently, was a man of peculiar eating habits who particularly enjoyed putting hot coleslaw on cantaloupe and hot gravy on apple pie.

He also had the most literal mind of any person I have ever encountered. "Tom, do you think it will stop raining?" writers in the press corp used to ask him, putting him on, whenever the heavens released a torrent.

"It always has," he invariably replied.

LEE ALLEN

Baseball writers work hard, but there is always a sense of playful companionship around them, because they must spend so much time together over the endless season and because they share the knowledge that they have all escaped doing something drearier and more serious in their lives.

ROGER ANGELL

A baseball writer, we all agree, is the lion of the sportswriting profession. But along about late July or early August, he starts to feel a lot more like one of those little hamsters in a revolving cage.

LEONARD KOPPETT

The most stupid ball player knows more, really, about the game than any baseball writer I ever knew.

JOHN KIERAN

Now, a World Series is a big thrill for a young baseball writer and for a baseball fan of any age, but for dotards like me it is just a golden opportunity to sit around and discuss the game as it was before Mr. Volstead substituted the lively ball for Schlitz in brown bottles.

> RING LARDNER

From my experience as a ghostwriter, I know that eventually the writer must fly solo. Assuming that the Babe tired, as most athletes do, it is necessary for the ghost to go the distance.

> JEROME HOLTZMAN, on Ford Frick's role in *Babe Ruth's Own Book of Baseball*

Joe, thanks for not trading me.

> JIM BUNNING, to Joe Falls after the Detroit columnist wrote about various trades that the Tigers should make

25

Radio and Television

The Game by Voice and Image . . .

Joe Garagiola on NBC television is today the fountain of all wisdom and knowledge. Woe to the player who makes a "head" mistake. Joe at length explains how the play should have been made, and how much the oversight cost the erring player's team. The "dumb" play is meat and potatoes for Garagiola, and what he doesn't criticize, his partner Tony Kubek does.

RED BARBER

All Kubek ever talks about is the Yankee club he once played on. You'd think no other club ever existed. Well, Kubek can hardly talk, so you can't expect him to interpret much.

BILLY ROGELL

You know what some of these advertising guys are trying to do? They're trying to get Diz to speak English.

PATRICIA DEAN

I often think of the roles everyone has in a telecast. But Jeff [Mitchell] is the one who expresses it best. He says, "I consider the announcers to be the authors of the television story, the players to be the actors, and myself and the crew to be the illustrators. They narrate the story and we put the pictures up there, and when we work well together, we have a hit show."

TIM McCARVER

"There's a word for what television's turned this game into."

"What's the word?"

"Beans," he said. "Nothing but beans and hot air."

WILLIAM LEAST HEAT MOON

The rain is coming down hard now. Although I guess the real story would be if the rain was going up.

TOMMY HUTTON, announcing a Yankee game

Would you say, Harvey, that this is the best game you ever pitched?

PITTSBURGH RADIO ANNOUNCER, after Harvey Haddix pitched a perfect game for twelve innings, only to lose by 1–0 in the thirteenth

When I said I was going to quit, Lylah [Barber], a very wise woman, said, "You don't have to quit tonight. You can do that tomorrow. . . . Let's have a martini."

RED BARBER, after learning from Branch Rickey that he intended to bring a black player into major league baseball

Televised baseball—particularly the network presentations—often seems to me to be moving at a faster pace than the game that is being covered: a curious business, to say the least. The silences of baseball and its quality of waiting, both inherent to the pastime, are habitually talked away by the announcers or twitched away by rapid camera cutting.

ROGER ANGELL

There was nobody I could have trusted more at that moment than these fatherly, familiar, and philosophical voices who'd already talked me through the minor disasters of a dozen summers. Lon [Simmons] and Bill [King] were magnificent. They proved they could joke their way through the apocalypse and also that baseball had taught them well about how to sort fact from conjecture.

JOHN KRICH, after the third game of the 1989 World Series was postponed because of an earthquake

26

Personalities

Assorted Ballplayers . . .

Henry Aaron

Photos of Aaron hitting homers baffled coaches. As the ball left his bat, his back foot was completely off the ground, all his weight was far forward, and—horror of horrors—his right hand flew off the bat an instant after contact, creating the illusion that he was swinging at the ball one-handed, almost throwing the bat at the ball.

THOMAS BOSWELL

The pitcher only had a ball, I had a bat.

HENRY AARON

What kind of player was he to manage? Just a dream—on and off the field.

BOBBY BRAGAN

Grover Cleveland Alexander

He could thread a needle with that ball. When he told you he was going to pitch a hitter a certain way and wanted you to play accordingly, you did it and that's all there was to it.

LES BELL

What's the use of doin' in three pitches what you can do in one?

GROVER CLEVELAND ALEXANDER

Dick Allen

Mays, Mantle, and Maris . . . but I saw Dick Allen. He was the best, just unbelievable.

GOOSE GOSSAGE

Walter Alston

He was a low-key manager that let his team play; he didn't act like he was the only one who could win or lose a game, like Billy Martin did.

QV LOWE

When I do get mad, I get too mad. I know this but I can't help myself.

WALT ALSTON

Ernie Banks

I saw right away that he was one of the nicest people in the game. And I could see that he could play.

HANK SAUER

I didn't know that Ernie Banks had any opinions except "Let's play at beautiful Wrigley Field."

JIM BROSNAN

Cool Papa Bell

I'll say this, going from first to home, Jesse [Owens] wouldn't have beaten Cool Papa [Bell]. Cool Papa was the fastest man I've ever seen. He was faster than Maury Wills and Lou Brock and Mickey Mantle when Mickey had good legs. He was faster than Bo Jackson and Kenny Lofton.

BUCK O'NEIL

Albert Belle

Albert honestly believes he's better than he is. He is very good and can be better. But almost no one on the planet is as good as Albert thinks he is.

MIKE HARGROVE

Johnny Bench

He came to the fore when the much smaller hinged catching mitt first became popular, and his shortstop-quick hands and his smoothness and balance and mobility behind the plate instantly caused all the catchers in the land to imitate his one-handed style, but none of them, then or now, could touch him.

ROGER ANGELL

Yogi Berra

Soon after I got traded to Baltimore, I came up to play in New York. Yogi [Berra] was the catcher, Eddie Rommel was the umpire, and I was the batter. I was trying to concentrate when I hear, "Hey, Gene, did you know Carmen's pregnant?" Rommel busted up. Yogi was serious, not trying to distract me. That was Yogi."

GENE WOODLING

"Yes, he *can* become a catcher."

BILL DICKEY

"Bill [Dickey] is learning me all his experiences."

YOGI BERRA

The players also felt that having Yogi around was like having a good-luck charm. Once we were on a plane that was bouncing through a thunderstorm. Lightning was dancing off the wings. Everyone was afraid, of course, but it was nothing like the chill we all felt when one wise guy remembered that Yogi had stayed back a few hours and taken a later flight. We said we could all see the picture of Yogi the next day with a sad look on his face as he was reading a newspaper headline that said, "YANKEE TEAM KILLED IN PLANE CRASH. BERRA LIVES CATCHES LATER FLIGHT." Whitey Ford said no, the headline would read, "MICKEY MANTLE, 26 OTHERS KILLED."

JIM BOUTON

Ping Bodie

I ain't bragging about myself or anything like that, but I got to admit I'm the only real ballplayer Connie [Mack]'s got. I and the Liberty Bell are the only attractions left in Philadelphia.

PING BODIE

Oil Can Boyd

He also had a Doberman that acquired a taste for beer! They both cut down, but how would you like to encounter a Doberman kicking a six-pack-a-day beer habit?

NOLAN RYAN

George Brett

And, best of all, George Brett batting, a brilliant repeated exhibit of precision and style and success.

ROGER ANGELL

Jim Brosnan

There was a limit to how much I could fit in. I was a good cook, but I wasn't going to discuss fine cuisine with another player. I wasn't going to ask any of the players to go with me to see Vladimir Horowitz in concert. I wasn't going to ask Bill Henry to come over and listen to Mahler. I never met anybody in baseball who liked classical music to the extent that I did. If they saw the ecstasy on my face they would have wondered what was wrong with me.

JIM BROSNAN

Three–Finger Brown

Mordecai, Mordecai, Mordecai Brown!
How come you goin' aroun' and aroun'?
"I heard the Yellow Pages talking:
'Let your fingers do the walking.'"

WILLIAM HARMON

Tommy Byrne

I'd like to have a buck for every time I was called a
"crazy left-hander" by somebody. How many times
have you ever heard somebody called a "crazy right-
hander"? That's discrimination. You ever see a left-
handed water fountain? There you are.

TOMMY BYRNE

Rod Carew

He'll have a three-ball, two-strike count on him and foul off six consecutive pitches. Then he'll finally let one go. Well, if he swung at six and didn't swing at that one, it's got to be ball four. The great hitters get treated that way because they've proven they know the strike zone. If Ted Williams didn't swing at a pitch, it was a ball, wherever it was.

RON LUCIANO

Steve Carlton

Carlton used to go into a trance-like state in the pen before he would warm up and I used to think he was just taking a nap. But what he was doing was visualizing the outside lane and the inside lane of the plate under the theory that thought precedes action and you keep the ball away from the fat part of the plate.

TIM McCARVER

Sometimes I hit him like I used to hit [Sandy] Koufax, and that's like drinking coffee with a fork.

WILLIE STARGELL

———————

Hugh Casey

Casey was a mean, rough man. It's an old line now in baseball, but I truly believe that if it meant something in a ball game Casey would not only have knocked his own mother down with a pitch, he would have hit her and in the head. He did not care for man or devil. He didn't even care for himself, as he proved several years later, after he was out of baseball, when he stuck a shotgun in his mouth, pulled the trigger, and blew himself into eternity.

RED BARBER

———————

Frank Chance

After a game lost this season Chance yelled at his men, "You're a fine lot of curs, you are." Not exactly the kind of talk boys expect from their fathers. Rumor has it that "curs" was not the word used, but it will do under the circumstances.

NEW YORK EVENING MAIL, July 24, 1908

Oscar Charleston

But the greatest ball player I've ever seen in my life was Oscar Charleston. I'd rate Oscar Charleston over Joe DiMaggio, over Willie Mays.

TED PAGE

If only I could calcimine him.

JOHN MCGRAW

Harry Chiti

Shortly after Harry Chiti was obtained by the Mets, he went to Stengel during an airplane trip and asked for permission to start a gin-rummy game. Stengel said no. He suggested that if Chiti, a catcher, had nothing to do he might go over the opposition hitters. Chiti went to sleep.

LEONARD SCHECTER

———•·•·•———

Roger Clemens

Sometimes he forgets that he's a human being. I have to remind him that even a pitching machine throws a bad one every once in a while.

BILL FISCHER

———•·•·•———

Roberto Clemente

He looked like he was falling apart when he ran. Looked like he was coming apart when he threw. His stance at the plate was ridiculous. When he swung he'd lunge and hit bad balls. There was no way he could hit the ball like that. But no one told Roberto that.

ROBIN ROBERTS

Some right fielders have rifles for arms, but he had a howitzer.

TIM MCCARVER

Ty Cobb

Thank goodness Al they ain't no Cobbs in this league and a man ain't scared of haveing his uniform stole off his back.

RING LARDNER

Ty Cobb was the fiercest competitor I ever saw on the field; he would do anything to beat you. But the nicest person to sit in the hotel lobby and visit with that you would ever want to meet. I could never put the two of them together. I used to listen to the great stories Cobb would tell, as we sat around the hotel lobbies, stories about base-stealing, and how they sharpened their spikes, as they did in those days. I was pleasantly surprised. He was very nice to me, he knew I was just a young kid.

RAY HAYWORTH

The greatest ballplayer I ever saw? Well, I'll have to say Ty Cobb. He could do more with a bat than any player of my time and I don't suppose there ever was a base runner like him. They tell you he wasn't much of a fielder, but he was good enough. I know he took a lot of base hits from me out there.

BABE RUTH

His foremost rival, Babe Ruth, had died in 1948 and an estimated quarter of a million people filed by his coffin at Yankee Stadium. The beloved Babe packed St. Patrick's Cathedral and every major-league club was represented at the two-day services. Ty Cobb drew just three men from big-league ball to his funeral. They were Mickey Cochrane, old-time catcher Ray Schalk, and Nap Rucker from his minor-league days.

AL STUMP

We were a lot alike. Our short move into the pitch was much the same. We were both place-hitters. We were lefties.

TRIS SPEAKER

I can pretty safely say that when Ty Cobb's mother blew her husband's brains out with a shotgun two weeks before Ty [Cobb]'s first big-league game, it might have had some effect on his personal development.

DAN GUTMAN

When Ty's Southern blood is aroused he is a bad man to handle.

HUGH JENNINGS

I don't think the fires ever went out in him, not till the day he died.

OSSIE BLUEGE

Was Ty Cobb psychotic throughout his baseball career? The answer is yes.

AL STUMP

Cobb is about as welcome in American League parks as a rattlesnake.

LOU GEHRIG

He was so great himself that he couldn't understand why if he told players how to do certain things, they couldn't do it as well as he did.

CHARLIE GEHRINGER

Players he had competed with and against did not visit him at Atherton in any number. Fred Haney, who had played with the Tigers, told of leaving a Detroit game with Cobb one evening in the mid-1940s and encountering players waiting for taxis. The boys were play-wrestling and laughing. "I wish I could have done that," said Cobb wistfully. "Had some pals on the team and kept them. But I didn't."

AL STUMP

Just before [Pete] Rose set the [lifetime] hit record in 1985, a reporter asked him, "Do you think Ty Cobb is up there looking down at you as you chase the record?"

Rose replied, "From what I know about the guy, he may not be up there. He may be down there."

DANIEL OKRENT AND STEVE WULF

Mickey Cochrane

I went up and singled to left, driving in the winning run. Cy [Perkins] took off his catching equipment just as the man crossed the plate, the boys on the bench told me much later, and said, "There goes Perkins' job on that base hit." I caught 135 that season.

MICKEY COCHRANE

Eddie Collins

[Ray Schalk said that] after Eddie Collins came to the White Sox in 1915, he became a better catcher. "Collins always caught the signal for a steal and gave me the sign. All I had to do was throw the ball to second base."

JAMES T. FARRELL

Bobby Cox

Sitting on the bench, Bobby Cox looks so aggravated on almost every play in a big game that you can't help but worry about his health. We once cut back from an antacid commercial to show the Braves' manager grimacing, and my quip was too easy: "The Battle of Mylanta."

TIM MCCARVER

Ray Dandridge

I made an appearance on the "Good Morning, America"show. [The announcer] said,"You know Whitey Ford had a good curve ball."

I told him, "I know Whitey Ford had one of the best curve balls. But I had one of the best bats."

RAY DANDRIDGE

Dizzy Dean

Every time I hold a ball in my hand and put that suit on. That's been my biggest day.

DIZZY DEAN

The Good Lord was good to me. He gave me a good body, a strong right arm and a weak mind.

DIZZY DEAN

"Damn it, get up to bat. He done give you the bunt sign three times."

DIZZY DEAN, while on the mound during a close game, to a rookie batter who stepped out of the box to check signals with the third base coach

By Judas Priest! By Judas Priest! If there were more like him in baseball, just one, as God is my witness, I'd get out of the game.

BRANCH RICKEY

X-RAYS OF DEAN'S HEAD SHOW NOTHING

HEADLINE IN DETROIT NEWSPAPER after Dizzy Dean was hit by thrown baseball in 1934 World Series

---

Martin DeHigo

DeHigo was the greatest all-round player I know. I say he was the best ball player of all time, black or white. He could do it all.

BUCK LEONARD

Bill Dickey

He was a great fellow to work with. He was real patient with a young pitcher, he'd always encourage you, and he seemed to know what to call for.

SPUD CHANDLER

Joe DiMaggio

They [Joe DiMaggio and Marilyn Monroe] had been married in January of that year, 1954, despite disharmony in temperament and time: he was tired of publicity, she was thriving on it; he was intolerant of tardiness, she was always late. During their honeymoon in Tokyo, an American general had introduced himself and asked if, as a patriotic gesture, she would visit the troops in Korea. She looked at Joe. "It's your honeymoon," he said, shrugging, "go ahead if you want to."

She appeared on ten occasions before 100,000 servicemen, and when she returned she said, "It was so wonderful, Joe. You never heard such cheering."

"Yes I have," he said.

GAY TALESE

I think he's as good as [Tris] Speaker ever was right now.

CLARK GRIFFITH

He was the greatest living ballplayer I've ever seen play.

YOGI BERRA

Moe Drabowsky

We were in the Oriole pen and it was about the sixth inning of the game. Jim Nash was pitching a two-hit shutout against us, just breezing. It wasn't really a premeditated thing on my part but I called over to their pen to find out what players were in the doghouse, whose wives were expecting babies, just get caught up on all the local news. When their coach, a fellow named Bobby Hofman, picked up the phone, I don't know why but I hollered, "Get Krausse hot in a hurry!" and hung up the phone. All of a sudden two bodies came charging out of the bullpen and they proceeded to heat up. Nash is still cruising along on this two-hitter and he looks down there and wonders what the hell is going on. So I let them throw for a while and then called back and said, "That's enough, sit 'em down."

MOE DRABOWSKY

Don Drysdale

I knocked down a lot of people but I can honestly say I never hit anybody in the head.

DON DRYSDALE

Leo Durocher

There was the time Lee Thomas went up to pinch-hit and Durocher sat on the bench saying, "Look at that bleep bleep bleep. He can't run, he can't hit, I don't know why the bleep bleep bleep I got him. Look at him! He's going to pop up." And sure enough, Thomas popped up. Durocher swore for several minutes, then turned to Ted Savage and told him to pinch-hit next. "Why should I go up there," said Savage, "and subject myself to abuse?"

ROY BLOUNT, JR.

I have never questioned the integrity of an umpire. Their eyesight, yes.

LEO DUROCHER

Durocher tried to intimidate the other team with this kind of rough stuff, but I think it backfired on him more often than not. He was just stirring up a nest of hornets. When Durocher came to town I was so charged up before the game, man, I could go out there and climb six fences. And I wasn't the only one. Our whole team was up.

STAN MUSIAL

Charlie Dressen

It's also true that Dressen talks too much, mostly in sentences beginning with "I," "I'm," or "I'll." (It should be remembered that he spent some of his formative days in the Three-I League.)

JOHN LARDNER

Jimmy Dykes

When I first came up, he would sit in the corner of the White Sox dugout and yell vicious insults. I'm sure he later let blacks have it, too. But he probably wasn't doing it as a racial thing. He was nasty to everybody.

GEORGE KELL

Bob Feller

The Cardinals and the Indians had an exhibition game in Cleveland. Feller was warming up and couldn't find homeplate. He was throwing the ball all over the place. Frankie Frisch, the St. Louis manager and second baseman, was a close observer of these proceedings. All of a sudden he turns to one of the utility infielders and says, "I don't feel so good today; you're playing second."

TONY PIET

Mark Fidrych

Fidrych's mother's parting words to him when he signed a pro contract were "You make sure you come home the same nut you've always been."

THOMAS BOSWELL

Whitey Ford

That was one thing you could count on with Whitey— he'd never make the same mistake twice. For a young fellow he was fantastic.

ED LOPAT

Whitey Ford said he had the hitter's front foot on a string and could jerk that lead foot off stride whenever he wanted.

THOMAS BOSWELL

Rube Foster

Oh no, he hasn't got a thing. I just thought he was shooting at me with a rifle when I was up there.

PERCY WERDEN

Everyone talks about how I campaigned for Cool Papa Bell and Rube Foster for the Hall of Fame, but I shouldn't have had to campaign for Rube Foster—he should have been the first.

TWEED WEBB

Jimmy Foxx

He had great powerful arms, and he used to wear his sleeves cut off way up, and when he dug in and raised that bat, those muscles would bulge and ripple.

TED LYONS

Frank Frisch

When they start speaking of second base-ing in particular, and bragging of the way second base is played in their time—TELL THEM ABOUT FRISCH.

Tell 'em most especially about the way Frisch played second base, some of center field and a slice of right field, too . . .

DAMON RUNYON

Lou Gehrig

I have a wonderful wife. I have a wonderful father and mother, and wonderful friends and teammates. I have been privileged to play many years with the famous Yankees, the greatest team of all times. All in all, I can say on this day that I consider myself the luckiest man on the face of the earth.

LOU GEHRIG, on Lou Gehrig Day, July 4, 1939, Yankee Stadium, two years before his death at age 38

It was commonly said at the time that Lou Gehrig lived in Ruth's shadow. Such talk never bothered Lou. "It's a pretty big shadow," he said. "It gives me lots of room to spread myself."

FRED LIEB

Bob Gibson

Solly [Hemus] also didn't like Bob Gibson. I don't think it was a black and white thing. He complained, "Bob throws every pitch at the same speed." That's like saying an atomic bomb explodes at the same velocity every time, so you can't use it.

TIM McCARVER

Josh Gibson

Who was the hardest hitter for me to pitch against? That's him: Josh Gibson. He could hit home runs around Babe Ruth's home runs. You look for his weakness, and while you're looking for it, he's liable to hit 45 home runs.

Satchel Paige

You couldn't fool him—don't think you're gonna fool him. Josh will hit you with one hand as quick as he will with two. I've seen him reach out on a sharp-breaking curveball on the outside from a right-hand pitcher, almost fooled him—almost. The ball almost got by him, and he reached out with one hand and hit it over the right field fence. And he ran the bases hollering, "Ha, you like to fooled me that time, but don't try that no more."

Verdell Mathis

Tom Glavine

I wanted to win this game as badly as any in my life, but I felt I had to fight my emotions and keep my ego in check.

> TOM GLAVINE, on letting Mark Wohlers pitch the ninth inning of the deciding game of the 1995 World Series for Atlanta

---

Lefty Gomez

I owe my baseball success to clean living and a fast outfield.

> LEFTY GOMEZ

Goose Goslin

Well, it was a great honor to win a batting title in those days. It wasn't an easy thing to do.

> GOOSE GOSLIN

Hank Greenberg

I was much more disappointed when I failed to break Gehrig's runs-batted-in record in 1937 then I was when I didn't break Babe Ruth's home-run record in 1938. Runs batted in were my obsession, not home runs.

HANK GREENBERG

Ken Griffey, Jr.

If he wants to he can hit 800 home runs.

FELIPE ALOU, after home run No. 350 at the age of 28

Lefty Grove

Here's this minor-league pitcher throwing nothing but fastballs and blowing them right past everybody. They knew what they were going to get, but it didn't make any difference. Somebody said, "Well, he'll never make it in the big league. All he can do is throw a fastball." And somebody else said, "Yeah, and all Galli-Curci can do is sing."

TED LYONS

Heinie Manush, a great hitter, was at bat with two men on the bases. The game was at stake, the count was three balls and two strikes. Heinie stood there, confident, looking for Lefty's fastball. "Well," thought Heinie, "it might be a curve." Lefty was throwing the curve more and more now, but the chances with the count of three and two were that Lefty would throw his fastball with everything he had on it. Fast or curve—he couldn't throw anything else, he had nothing else to throw. Heinie broke his bat striking out on the next pitch, the first forkball Lefty ever threw.

MOE BERG

Tony Gwynn

He's going to get his hits and you just hope no one's on base. He has such a short, compact swing and such a good idea of the strike zone that you are not going to fool him very often. Out of 650 at bats in a season you will fool him maybe ten times.

MIKE LaVALLLIERE

Being a hitter, I hate to see a no-hitter (or worse a perfect game), but once again you just have to sit back and applaud.

TONY GWYNN

Rickey Henderson

I am the captain of the outfield.

RICKEY HENDERSON

Rogers Hornsby

He comes into the clubhouse and gets into his uniform and goes out and plays the ball game. When the game is over, he takes his shower and dresses and goes out and we don't see him again until the next day. Nobody knows where he goes or where he lives or what he does between ball games, because he don't talk to anybody except during a ball game, and then he don't talk much.

FERDIE SCHUPP

"Did you ever pitch much to Rogers Hornsby, Red?" I asked [Red Faber].

"I struck him out. It was at an old-timers game at Comiskey Park."

"Yes," Ray Schalk remarked, "and Lefty Gomez on the bench said, 'After twenty-five years we learned how to pitch to him.'"

JAMES T. FARRELL

I hit .361, played second base, and managed the club on two western trips. What does a fellow have to do to stay in New York?

ROGERS HORNSBY, upon being traded by the Giants to the Boston Braves

It's nice. Now get it outta here so we can start the game.

ROGERS HORNSBY, upon being presented with a new Cadillac on Rogers Hornsby Day at Beaumont, Texas

Hornsby, wrote the Boston columnist Austen Lake shortly after his death, "was as addicted to the truth as a drunk was to his bottle." A cynic might have added that he was at least as addicted to horse-playing as he was to the truth.

CHARLES C. ALEXANDER

Ralph Houk

Houk tried to look comfortable in his new role [as Yankees' general manager], but mostly he looked out of place, or as one player said, "like a whore in church."

JIM BOUTON

Carl Hubbell

Well, it would be kinda hard to answer that because Nolan Ryan won't be pitching against Ruth, Gehrig, Foxx, Simmons, and Cronin.

> CARL HUBBELL, at the 1979 All-Star Game, upon being asked whether he thought Ryan could equal his feat of striking out in order the five leading hitters in the American League lineup of 1934

You could catch him in a rocking chair. He had two important requirements: good control and a good disposition.

BOB O'FARRELL

I'll tell you something about Hubbell. When he was pitching, you hardly ever saw the opposing team sitting back in the dugout; they were all up on the top step, watching him operate. He was a marvel to watch, with that screwball, fastball, curve, screwball again, change of speed, control. He didn't really have overpowering stuff, but he was an absolute master of what he did have, and he got every last ounce out of his abilities.

BILLY HERMAN

Shoeless Joe Jackson

Jackson never seemed to know whether the pitcher was left-handed or right, or whether he hit a fastball, curve, a spitter, or any of the trick deliveries. All he'd say, if you asked him, was that the ball was over. 'Over' for Jackson meant anything he could reach.

JACK GRANEY

For Shoeless Joe is gone, long gone,
A long yellow grass-blade between his teeth
And the bleacher shadows behind him

NELSON ALGREN

Joe Jackson's not alive any more. He's served his sentence, and it's time for baseball to acknowledge his debt is paid; and the Hall of Fame Committee on Veterans to list him as a nominee.

TED WILLIAMS

Reggie Jackson

I represent both the underdog and the overdog in our society.

REGGIE JACKSON

Another time Reggie [Jackson] was giving Mickey Rivers the same jive. "My IQ is 160," he told Mickey. Mickey looked at Reggie and said, "Out of what, Buck, a thousand?"

SPARKY LYLE

Derek Jeter

All I ever wanted to be was a Yankee. When I was a kid I was always hoping there'd be a jersey left for me to wear with a single digit.

DEREK JETER, who wears No. 2

Randy Johnson

[Randy Johnson] long had been the kind of natural wonder better suited to an Ansel Adams portrait than a baseball card.

TOM VERDUCCI

Walter Johnson

He says what was the matter with Johnson's work? I says he ain't got nothing but a fastball. Then he says Yes and Rockefeller ain't got nothing but a hundred million bucks.

RING LARDNER

Didn't even have a curve. Just that fast ball. That's all he pitched, just fast balls. He didn't need any curve.

SAM CRAWFORD

He had what I would describe as a slingshot delivery. It was a nice, easy movement, which didn't seem to be putting any strain at all on his arm. But he could propel that ball like a bullet.

FRED LINDSTROM

Addie Joss

It was then that the great Master of the Universe took the star twirler out of the box and sent him to the clubhouse . . .

THE REV. BILLY SUNDAY, funeral sermon for Addie Joss, Toledo, Ohio, 1911

George Kell

I knew that [Art Houtteman] was stubborn enough to test his fastball against me although I was a good fastball hitter. So on the first pitch I guessed correctly that he'd challenge me with his best fastball down the middle. I jumped all over it and drilled it for a double off the wall. As I glided into second, Art looked at me and said, "You really can hit a fastball, Cap'n."

GEORGE KELL

Sandy Koufax

All at once Sandy got control. And I don't mean control in the sense of just throwing the ball over the plate. He could throw the fastball where he wanted to—to spots. When you have that kind of stuff and that kind of control, well, they just stopped hitting him. And it all happened in one year.

WALTER ALSTON

Napoleon Lajoie

It may be true that Larry's through, he may be going back;

But if you think he's on the blink, just talk to Connie Mack.

W. H. HOEFFER

Buck Leonard

Trying to sneak a fastball past him was like trying to sneak a sunrise past a rooster.

MONTE IRVIN

Sparky Lyle

I remember one day before a game, [Bill] Virdon called a team meeting to go over the hitters. We were playing Baltimore, and Fred Stanley had gotten a casket from a guy in the business, an economy one with white silk, silver sprayed. It was finished inside, and Fred was going to make a bar out of it for his van. When he got it, he brought it into the clubhouse and kept it there until he could ship it home. It was sitting on a hand truck in the middle of the room. Well, I had gotten a surgical mask from a friend of mine. It had a hood that fit over your head, and all you could see were your eyes. I got lampblack and put it around my eyes and got them real black. Before the meeting started, I laid down inside the casket and shut it. I was listening, and Bill was going over the Baltimore lineup, and all of a sudden I lifted the top of the casket and said, "How dooooooo yooooooo pitch to Brooks Ro—been—son?"

SPARKY LYLE

Connie Mack

He could be uncanny. We had Ty Cobb playing with us in '27 and '28, his last two years in baseball. One day he's in right field and Connie starts moving him over with the scorecard, keeps moving him and moving him. You could tell from the way Cobb was responding out there that he thought this was all very curious. But he went along with Connie. Well, the batter hit the ball right at him. He never had to move. When he came in to the bench at the end of the inning, Cobb said to Connie, "I've heard a lot about your scorecard, and from now on I'm going to believe in it."

JIMMY DYKES

Connie entered professional baseball when it was a game for roughnecks. He saw it become respectable, he lived to be symbol of its integrity, and he enjoyed every minute of it.

RED SMITH

Greg Maddux

Greg Maddux is the prime example of a fast worker. . . . Maddux is the type of guy who would have told Lincoln to hurry up his Gettysburg Address or told Chopin to shorten his "Minute Waltz."

TIM MCCARVER

He doesn't seem dominating, then you look up on the scoreboard and you've got one hit and it's the eighth inning.

JIM THOME

Mickey Mantle

We sometimes seem to save our greatest devotion for those heroes who don't quite make it, or who lose gallantly, or who have flaws. Mantle more than fit the image.

ROBERT W. CREAMER

That boy hits balls over buildings. He runs as fast as Ty Cobb.

CASEY STENGEL

Juan Marichal

But the best pitcher I ever batted against was Juan Marichal, because he threw so many goddam different kinds of good pitches against you.

PETE ROSE

Rube Marquand

Sooner or later he'd get around to the game he liked best to recall. It was against the Pirates, always a soft touch for him. "Just get me one run," he told his teammates. "That's all I need to beat these guys."

It was tied until the 21st when Larry Doyle hit an inside-the-park homer. "Next time you say you need only one run to win," laughed Larry, "be specific. Name the inning."

JOE WILLIAMS

Billy Martin

Martin was "tendency-prone," but he had so many tendencies it was hard to predict what he would do next.

GEORGE F. WILL

Pepper Martin

We were put out of hotels in other cities, too. The Governor Clinton for one. They had a big wind fan there that cooled off the whole lobby, and Pepper strolled over in front of it with some sneezing powder folded into the crease of his newspaper. He opened the paper, and well . . . the whole lobby was cleaned out in two minutes. Bar and all.

LEO DUROCHER

Christy Mathewson

I attribute much of my success to my ability to get most of the compelling force from the swing of the body.

CHRISTY MATHEWSON

I believe he could have continued to pitch shoutouts until Christmas.

> GRANTLAND RICE, after Mathewson's third shutout in the 1905 World Series

Be it recorded here, New York possesses the pitching marvel of the century . . .

> NEW YORK TIMES, Oct. 15, 1905

Eddie Mathews

I've only known three or four perfect swings in my time. This boy's got one of them.

> TY COBB

Willie Mays

Always try for perfection. There's never been a perfect ball player. Willie Mays came closest. But always try.

> JOE DIMAGGIO

That Willie Mays, he's one of the greatest center fielders who ever lived. You can go back as far as you want and name all the great ones—Tris Speaker, Eddie Roush, Max Carey, Earl Combs, Joe DiMaggio. I don't care who you name, Mays is just as good, maybe better.

HARRY HOOPER

Only a handful of players, in all baseball history, have been as important to winning teams, and have been able to contribute as much to eventual victory, rather than to statistics, as has Mickey Mantle. Willie, on the other hand, I can sum up very simply: he's the best baseball player I ever saw.

LEONARD KOPPETT

Willie Mays had the most unsurpassed instinct or anticipation I've ever seen. You could just concentrate on him on the ballfield—be watching him, and I say, by looking, seeing— you see the ball going to the plate, you actually see a ball hit, and it looked as though simultaneously with the bat touching the ball, Mays was moving. It was phenomenal.

CHARLIE FOX

Willie liked to extend his arms like Duke Snider, Mickey Mantle, and other power hitters, so if you crowded him with one pitch and then threw a pitch low and away you could give him trouble. Of course, you could pitch God that way, and it would give Him trouble.

DON NEWCOMBE

"Willie," they asked, "how do you compare this catch with other catches you've made?"
"I don't compare 'em," Willie said. "I catch 'em."

LEO DUROCHER

I'm not sure just what the hell charisma is, but I get the feeling it's Willie Mays.

TED KLUSZEWSKI

Joe McCarthy

Red Rolfe was originally a shortstop, too, but he didn't have the real good arm for making that long throw. I told him I was going to play him at third base.

"It's one of the easiest jobs in the infield," I told him. "You average about three chances a game. And don't worry about those hot smashes. That's a big joke. You've got a glove and you can stop them."

"Okay," he said.

He broke in at third up at Fenway Park. The first ball hit down to him took a bad bounce and hit him in the eye and blackened it. He came into the dugout holding his eye and said, "Joe, you gave me some bad information." But he became a good third baseman.

JOE McCARTHY

I'd worry if I were 30 games ahead.

JOE McCARTHY.

He always had a reason for everything he did.

SPUD CHANDLER

Looking out at the wavering farmhouse lights, ones which rushed through the darkened landscape, McCarthy had paused and said, "You know, Case [Stengel], that's the life for me. Nothing to worry about except get up and do the milking. Sometimes I think I'm in the greatest business in the world. Then you lose four straight and want to change places with the farmer."

CURT SMITH

In the clubhouse there was usually a lot of frivolity and fun. But when Joe [McCarthy] walked in the door that was the end of it.

ED WELLS

Listen, any manager who can't get along with a .400 hitter ought to have his head examined.

JOE MCCARTHY, on becoming Ted Williams's manager

Sam McDowell

The Cleveland Indians' great fastballer, Sudden Sam McDowell, would start complaining even before he released his pitch. "Ball?" he'd screech, then release it— "How can that be a ball?"

RON LUCIANO

John McGraw

If you made a bad play he'd say, "Son, come over here and sit down by me." You'd do that and he would say, "Now, why did you make that play that way?" Usually the fellow would say, "I thought—" and McGraw would interrupt and say, "With what? You just do the playing. I'll do the thinking for this club."

BURLEIGH GRIMES

It's curious the grip that McGraw gets on you. No one could have been nicer to me than Jack Hendricks was when I was with the Reds, nor than Joe McCarthy was when I was with the Cubs. But when I had a ball player I knew would make the big leagues, I had to give him to McGraw although I hadn't spoken to Mac for six years.

ART NEHF

He combined the endearing personal traits of George Steinbrenner and Billy Martin—he was arrogant, combative, aggressive, insolent, cocksure, skillful, quick to take advantage, quick to take offense—and, like Steinbrenner and Martin, he was successful, a winner or close to it year after year.

ROBERT W. CREAMER

But although [McGraw] wanted his Giants to play rough and tough, they had to be gentlemen off the field. He elevated the status of the ball player, getting his ball club into the best hotels.

BOG BROEG

McGraw loved to attack opposing pitchers best—by showering them with low-blow insults. Once, during a game in Philadelphia, Phillies pitcher Ad Brennan decided he had heard enough slurs from the obnoxious Giants manager. Brennan called time, left the mound, walked coolly over to the Giants dugout, and coldcocked McGraw with one punch. In gratitude, fans the next day presented Brennan with a huge bouquet of flowers.

BRUCE WARD AND ALLAN ZULLO

Mark McGwire

McGwire looks like the Babe's heir, an absolute monster of a man, and yet like Ruth so obviously warm and gentle. McGuire's home runs do not merely clear the fences. They are not parabolas. Rather they just go out until they run into something.

FRANK DEFORD

The great majority of bats are supplied to major-league batters by Rawlings, Louisville Slugger, Hoosier, and, in the case of Mark McGwire, the NASA Jet Propulsion Laboratory.

TIM MCCARVER

Joe Medwick

The trouble with that Medwick is, he don't talk none, he just hits you.

DIZZY DEAN

Bob Meusel

He didn't learn to say hello until it was time to say goodbye.

FRANK GRAHAM, on Meusel's affability during his final season, after years of surliness to sportswriters

Stan Musial

When I was young I would listen to my subconscious, and my subconscious would always tell me what the pitcher was trying to do.

STAN MUSIAL

Before Willie Mays's first appearance against the Cardinals, Leo Durocher ran down the St. Louis batting order for him, telling the rookie how the various batters should be played. He described the lead-off batter, and the number two man, and then moved to the clean-up hitter.

Mays interrupted to ask about number three.

"The third hitter," Durocher said, "is Stan Musial. There is no advice I can give you about him."

DANIEL OKRENT AND STEVE WULF

Bobo Newsom

This is Bobo's fifth term in Washington, which makes Bobo one up on Roosevelt.

BOBO NEWSOM, after signing once again with the Senators

Commissioner of Baseball Kenesaw M. Landis once tried to explain to Newsom why he wanted him to stop playing the horses. "Damn it, Newsom," the Judge said, "a ballplayer who bets the horses can't keep his mind on baseball. Suppose you're pitching in a tight game and you have to bat in the ninth inning at just about the same time a horse you have a big bet on is running at the track. What will you be thinking of, the ball game or your bet?"

To which Newsom replied, "Mr. Commissioner, you don't have to worry about a thing. If it's a tight ball game in the ninth inning, they sure as hell won't have ol' Bobo up there hittin'."

ROBERT W. CREAMER

Sadaharu Oh

Mr. Kojiru Suzuki threw a sinker on the outside part of the plate. I followed the ball perfectly. I could almost feel myself waiting for its precise break before I let myself come forward. When I made contact, I felt like I was scooping the ball outward and upward. The ball rose slowly and steadily in the night sky, lit by Korakuen's bright lights. I could follow it all the way as it lazily reached its height and seemed to linger there in the haze, and then slowly began its descent into the right-field stands.

SADAHARU OH

Mel Ott

Ott is a standout with me. Ott is the best-looking young player at the bat, in my time with the club.

JOHN MCGRAW

Joe Page

He had one of the great left arms, he had the guts of a burglar and for emergencies he kept a supply of graphite oil on the inner side of his belt.

RED SMITH

Satchel Paige

Satch didn't get into the majors by throwin' the ball over the plate. He made it by throwin' it over a matchbook in the center of the plate.

COOL PAPA BELL

He would throw the ball on the corner just far enough so if you would swing, you couldn't get all the way around on it. Control. What you don't see in the big leagues now.

JUDY JOHNSON

It's like I said at Satchel [Paige]'s funeral in 1982: people say it's a shame he never pitched against the best. But who's to say he didn't?

BUCK O'NEIL

Jim Palmer

Once, seeing Palmer reading *Dr. Zhivago*, teammate Steve Stone said, "It must be about an elbow specialist."

THOMAS BOSWELL

I have to move my outfielders ten steps to the right, so that after Palmer moves them back five steps to the left, they'll end up in the right place.

EARL WEAVER

Gaylord Perry

I don't take one thing away from him for winning three hundred with the spitter. There are loopholes in the rules and you get away with what you can.

DON BAYLOR

Dusty Rhodes

Call me Liberace.

DUSTY RHODES, September, 1954, upon returning to the Giants' bench after striking out, having declared that he was going to get a hit off the Brooklyn Dodger's rookie pitcher Karl Spooner "or I'll kiss your ass"

Hey, George, flip me one of them hanging curves.

DUSTY RHODES, to George Spencer during batting practice

Bobby Richardson

He don't smoke, he don't drink, and he still can't hit .250.

CASEY STENGEL

Cal Ripken, Jr.

"Cal Ripken," [Orioles General Manager Roland] Hemond said, "plays the infield like a manager." By this he meant that Ripken is a cerebral player, constantly moving in response to the changed situation, from pitch to pitch, in anticipation of what his pitcher will do, which depends on what the pitcher expects the batter to expect (which depends on what the batter thinks the pitcher expects him to expect).

GEORGE F. WILL

Am I proud of him? Well, sure I'm proud of him as my son. But as a ballplayer, ask in fifteen years.

CAL RIPKEN, SR., on Cal Ripken, Jr., at age 22

Robin Roberts

I had a fine right arm and a great delivery, but I pitched too much and wore myself down. I wasn't quite selfish enough or smart enough.

ROBIN ROBERTS

———•••••———

Brooks Robinson

Make it rain, Brooksie.

FELLOW ORIOLE PLAYER after another spectacular play at third base during the 1970 World Series

He belongs in a higher league.

PETE ROSE, during 1970 World Series

———•••••———

Frank Robinson

I know 91 pitchers and 9 managers in the league who will chip in $500 apiece if [Frank] Robinson will go through on his plans to retire. That's $50,000 for him.

GENE MAUCH

Jackie Robinson

Mr. Rickey, I've got to do it.

> JACKIE ROBINSON, when asked by Branch Rickey whether he could take the abuse he would receive upon being the first black player in the major leagues, without fighting back

We didn't think he was the best. He ran well and he was a fighter, but he wasn't one of the Negro "stars." It just goes to show you that you can't always tell about a ballplayer. Branch Rickey saw something there and he was right. Robinson was the man for the job, college-educated, a winner, a man with good self-control.

BUCK LEONARD

You saw how he stood there at the plate and dared them to hit him with the ball and you began to put yourself in his shoes. You'd think of yourself trying to break in the black leagues maybe, and what it would be like—and I know that I couldn't have done it. In a word: he was winning respect.

PEE WEE REESE

Why don't you guys go to work on somebody who can fight back? There isn't one of you has the guts of a louse.

EDDIE STANKY, to Philadelphia Phillies riding Jackie Robinson in 1947

The [Brooklyn] team is in Pittsburgh. I walk into the Forbes Field dressing room carrying my duffel bag. Just inside the door Jackie Robinson comes over, sticks out his hand, and says, "After I hit against you in spring training, I knew you'd be up here. I didn't know when, but I knew it would happen. Welcome." . . . I'd have been grateful if anyone had said "Hello." And to get this from not just any ballplayer but from Jackie Robinson.

CARL ERSKINE

Joe Rogan

They ought to put some of those [black] guys in the Hall of Fame, I told Casey Stengel, "The guys they put in the Hall of Fame are a joke. [Bullet Joe] Rogan's the guy ought to go in." Casey recommended it to the commissioner, but it never took.

BABE HERMAN

———

Pete Rose

Everyone seemed to love Pete the player: the fans, the writers, the umpires, the managers, the ground crew, everyone associated with the game. We respected him so much that we sometimes forgot to assess his playing skills adequately. No one ever said that about Cobb. No one said that Cobb was the kind of guy they would have enjoyed playing with, that he brought out the best in you. No one ever said that they respected Cobb so much that they forgot how good he was.

CRAIG R. WRIGHT

One of the game's greatest players has engaged in a variety of acts which have stained the game, and he must now live with the consequences of those acts.

A. BARTLETT GIAMATTI

I don't think Pete Rose deserves to be in the Hall of Fame because he was offered a chance to come clean, and he didn't come clean. He has never really admitted that he did something wrong. He has never really come right out and said, "Yes, I'm guilty [of betting on baseball games in which he played and managed]. And I'm just sorry for the whole thing."

MONTE IRVIN

Al Rosen

But the key moment in the Yankees '51 campaign came in a critical September game against Cleveland at Yankee Stadium before a crowd of 68,000, with the score tied in the ninth, DiMaggio on third, and Phil Rizzuto, then the game's most accomplished bunter, at the plate. The combination of Rizzuto's special talent and DiMaggio's skill as a runner made the game-winning squeeze play foreordained. "Tell me," DiMaggio said idly to Al Rosen, the Cleveland third baseman. "Do you think he's going to bunt?" "I'll be the most surprised Jew in the place if he doesn't," Rosen responded. In the outcome, Rosen was not surprised.

CHARLES EINSTEIN

Babe Ruth

A rabbit didn't have to think to know what to do to dodge a dog. Instinct told him. The same kind of instinct told [Babe] what to do and where to be. . . . I never heard anybody tell him anything to do on the ball field.

SAM VICK

A theory had been advanced that because Ruth was such a pronounced pull hitter, he could be stopped if he were given nothing but low outside pitches. Chicago's Eddie Cicotte tested the theory and Ruth hit three successive doubles to the opposite field. The next day he hit another double and two triples. End of theory.

ROBERT W. CREAMER

Wives of ball players, when they teach their children their prayers, should instruct them to say: "God bless Mommy, God bless Daddy, God bless Babe Ruth! Babe has upped daddy's home pay check by 15 to 40 percent!"

WAITE HOYT

Not many pitchers I interviewed had trouble with Ruth, because they kept the ball low and away from him. It makes one wonder off of whom he hit those 714 home runs?

EUGENE MURDOCK

He had a heap of living to do to make up for the grim years of his youth. And he never thought there would be an end to his skills.

CLAIRE MERRITT HODGSON RUTH

I knew Ruth couldn't hit with me—that is, real batting—or run bases with me—or (play) outfield with me.

TY COBB

[Ruth] and Ping Bodie got along well. They were roommates and often ate together. Bodie had been considered the biggest eater on the [Yankee] club before Ruth came along, but now he admitted defeat. "Anybody who eats three pounds of steak and a bottle of chili sauce for a starter has got me," he said.

ROBERT W. CREAMER

Because of Ruth's bulk, [Jacob] Ruppert decided to dress the Yankees in the now-traditional pinstripe uniform and dark blue stockings. The natty, clothes-conscious Ruppert felt the new uniform would make Babe look trimmer. The Yankees also introduced uniform numbers to the major leagues in 1929. Ruth's number was number 3 because he batted third, Gehrig's 4 because he batted fourth, and so on.

ROBERT W. CREAMER

You know, I saw it all happen, from beginning to end. But sometimes I still can't believe what I saw: this nineteen-year-old kid, crude, poorly educated, only lightly brushed by the social veneer we call civilization, gradually transformed into the idol of American youth and the symbol of baseball the world over—a man loved by more people and with an intensity of feeling that perhaps has never been equaled before or since. I saw a man transformed from a human being into something pretty close to a god.

HARRY HOOPER

One day the Babe took the wrong way on the road to some golf club.

"Hey, this is a one-way street," the traffic cop hollered.

"I'm only driving one way, you dumb _____," the Babe said. The cop, enraged, came running up. "Oh, hello, Babe," he said. "I didn't know it was you. Drive any way you want to."

GRANTLAND RICE

He was easy to like and was at his best in the clutch. To me he was the most exciting player to watch of all time.

BILL DICKEY

I'm going to wait until I get formal notice. Leave Judge Landis make the first move. I'm going to leave it lie.

BABE RUTH, on being suspended for taking part in a prohibited exhibition tour

There are a lot of people who would rather watch Babe Ruth hit a long fly than see Hack Wilson smack the ball over the garden wall. One is an artist, the other a plumber.

JOE WILLIAMS

Ruth was calming down rapidly [after invading the Giants' clubhouse], and when one of McGraw's coaches told him he'd better leave he said, "All right. I know I shouldn't have come in here, but I wanted to get things straight. Listen, I'm sorry, fellows. Tomorrow, let's cut out the rough stuff and just play baseball."

Heinie Groh, the Giants' third baseman, hooted. The day before, Ruth had slid into Groh like a fullback hitting the line. "Baseball?" said Groh. "Look who's talking. Yesterday I thought we were playing football."

Everybody laughed. Ruth and [Bob] Meusel started to go, but at the door Babe turned back for a moment. "Don't get me wrong, fellows," he said seriously. "I don't mind being called a prick or a cocksucker or things like that. I expect that. But lay off the personal stuff."

ROBERT W. CREAMER

Despite the rain, the day was hot and humid, and after the honorary pallbearers took a last look at the body of America's foremost athlete, one of the ex-Yankees, Joe Dugan, whispered, "I surely would like to have a big glass of beer." "So would the Babe," whispered Waite Hoyt.

FRED LIEB

Nolan Ryan

I was looking for a fastball, he threw a curve and I got vapor-locked.

BRAD MILLS, after becoming Nolan Ryan's 4000th strikeout victim

---

Johnny Sain

Johnny Sain loves pitchers. Maybe he doesn't love base-ball so much, but he loves pitchers. Only he understands them.

MICKEY LOLICH

Mike Schmidt

During a game, Schmidt brings such formidable attention and intelligence to bear on the enemy pitcher that one senses that the odds have almost been reversed out there: it is the man on the mound, not the one up at the plate, who is in worse trouble from the start.

ROGER ANGELL

Tom Seaver

I learned to let my talent dictate what I was on a given day. I learned to adjust to it, its limits, to what it told me about myself. I couldn't do more than I was physically or mentally capable of. If I tried to throw harder than I could, the ball went slower than it normally would.

TOM SEAVER

Ernie Shore

No, I wasn't nervous. Why should I have been? There were only three things that could happen—I could win, I could lose, or I could tie.

ERNIE SHORE, on starting a World Series game

George Sisler

For that one year (1922) at least he must have been the most remarkable ball player we ever saw . . .

ALLISON DANZIG

Ozzie Smith

He gets up like a cat.

DAVE CONCEPCION

Ozzie Smith just made another play that I've never seen anyone else make before, and I've seen him make it more than anyone else ever has.

JERRY COLEMAN

Sammy Sosa

My career has been very successful . . . but nobody remembers that Sammy Sosa had to work very hard and cried many tears. This is an important thing betweeen us Latinos.

SAMMY SOSA

THERE MAY BE SLIGHT DELAYS WHEN SAMMY SOSA'S AT BAT.

CHICAGO TRANSIT AUTHORITY sign near elevated train stop at Wrigley Field, 1998

Bezball been berry, berry good to me!

SAMMY SOSA

Warren Spahn

I don't think Spahn will ever get into the Hall of Fame. He'll never stop pitching.

STAN MUSIAL

Tris Speaker

He simply did everything well. I don't think you could ask for a better all-around ball player.

SMOKY JOE WOOD

———

George Stallings

Only once did Stallings forget the name of a car owned by one of his players. Seeking to call attention to the mental shortcomings of [Hank] Gowdy, who missed a sign one day, the Braves' manager turned to the rest of the bench.

"Look at him up there," he spattered derisively, "the—the—"And there was a pause as Stallings tried in vain to recall the name of the car driven by Gowdy. He was stumped, but not for long.

"Look at him," yelled Stallings, "the bicycle-riding so-and-so."

TOM MEANY

Eddie Stanky

He can't run, he can't hit and he can't throw. But if there's a way to beat the other team, he'll find it.

BRANCH RICKEY

Willie Stargell

I think if you have a leader like a Willie Stargell on your team you're all right.

ROBIN ROBERTS

Casey Stengel

He could make a sick monkey laugh.

BOB SMITH

A few days later when he failed to slide and was tagged out, the crowd hooted as he returned to the dugout. There weren't many people in the stands, and it wasn't hard to hear him when he paused before going into the dugout, looked up at the crowd, and said, "With the salary I get I'm so hollow and starving that if I slide I'm liable to explode like a light bulb."

ROBERT W. CREAMER

Wake up, muscles! We're in New York now!

CASEY STENGEL, when traded to the Giants in 1921, and while slapping himself on the chest, arms and legs

The paths of glory lead but to the Braves.

CASEY STENGEL, upon being traded to Boston after his outstanding 1923 World Series for the New York Giants

Now, you boys haven't been playing very well, but I know there's been a lot on your minds. I see a lot of you reading about the stock market, and I know you're thinking about it. Now, I'm going to do you a favor, since you're so interested in Wall Street. I'm going to give you a tip on the market. (Pause.) Buy Pennsylvania Railroad. (Pause.) Because (—whack!—) if you don't start playing better ball there's gonna be so many of you riding trains out of here that railroad stocks are a cinch to go up.

CASEY STENGEL, to the Toledo Mud Hens, 1929

Casey Stengel is said to have watched a long drive to center go past his center fielder, and bounce around behind the three monuments [in Yankee Stadium] while his outfielder had troubles picking it up. Finally, Casey yelled, "Ruth, Gehrig, Huggins—somebody throw the ball."

PHILIP J. LOWRY

"You are retiring of your own volition, aren't you, Mr. Stengel?" asked [Dan] Topping. There was a moment of silence in which you could have heard a pin drop. Then Stengel, raising his voice, electrified the session by saying crisply, "Boys, I'm not retiring; I've just been fired." On this low note ended Stengel's magnificent career with the Yankees.

FRED LIEB

You couldn't fool Casey because he'd pulled every stunt that was ever thought up, and he did it fifty years before we even got there.

MICKEY MANTLE.

I got this broken arm from watching my team. We're improving magnificently. All they gave me last year was a head cold.

CASEY STENGEL, on the New York Mets

That [World Series] ring don't cost so much. I got four or five rings and don't know whether I'm going to wear five of them when I go out. Unless you're broke, the ring is the best thing you can get which money comes in handy all the time. If a player don't shoot he can go and play against us which is all right in the first place too. The situation is for five years and they still haven't found the end of it, the other guys. They say the owners are rich, so what? We must have the umpires, not the same ones. It's the money the Yankees got. On the ball club you can't write it all down. You do it. So they say it's the lively ball and the damn bunting. . . . What about the shortstop Rizzuto who got nothing but daughters but throws out the left-handed hitters in the double play?

CASEY STENGEL

Everybody knows that Casey [Stengel] has forgotten more baseball than I'll ever know. That's the trouble, he's forgotten it.

JIMMY PIERSALL

There was one criticism of Stengel that was more legitimate than most. He did have a tendency to force an injured man to play, to overuse a hot pitcher, to sacrifice an individual's welfare for the smell of victory. This form of selfishness is not the most admirable trait in the world—but it can be doubted that many successful generals throughout the history of mankind were free of it.

LEONARD KOPPETT

Frank Sullivan

I'm in the twilight of a mediocre career.

FRANK SULLIVAN

Don Sutton

I ought to get a Black and Decker commercial out of it.

DON SUTTON, on his reputation for scuffing up baseballs

Gene Tenace

It was unbelievable. I had just been trying to make contact. But I'll be darned if it didn't go out. I started around the bases and when I was turning second base I thought I'd look for my folks in the crowd. I knew about where they were sitting, in the third-base boxes. Sure enough, there was my father, jumping up and down and applauding and yelling. With it being a Cincinnati crowd there weren't too many people doing that, and I guess that's how I was able to spot him. I caught his eye and for those few seconds we were looking at each other. It was a great feeling.

GENE TENACE

Bill Terry

Art for art's sake, or baseball without a dignified salary, were not for Bill Terry.

W. P. KINSELLA

The son of a bitch was some kind of hitter.

TED WILLIAMS

—•••—

Gorman Thomas

The frowsy Thomas was a walking strip mine; he had worn the same pair of uniform stockings, now as threadbare as the Shroud of Turin, since opening day of 1978. I recall a moment in the Brewer clubhouse during the Series when a group of us were chatting with Thomas's father—he was the retired postmaster of Charleston, South Carolina—and some genius reporter asked what Gorman's room had looked like back when he was a teen-ager. "Turrible!" Thomas père said, wincing at the thought. "Why, I could hahdly make myself look in theah!"

ROGER ANGELL

—•••—

Bobby Thomson

It was the most famous home run ever made. He hit it in 3,000,000 living rooms, to say nothing of the bars and grills.

GARRY SCHUMACHER, on Bobby Thomson's pennant-winning home run for the Giants in 1951

Bob Uecker

If Bob Uecker had not been on the Cardinals, then it's questionable whether we could have beaten the Yankees [in 1964]. He kept everything so funny that we never had the chance to think of what a monumental event we were playing in, against the New York Yankees of all teams.

TIM McCARVER

Mo Vaughn

That's all I do is hit. It's all I think about every day. This ain't no fluke here.

MO VAUGHN

Rube Waddell

He had more stuff than any pitcher I ever saw. He had everything but a sense of responsibility.

CONNIE MACK

Honus Wagner

Nobody ever saw anything graceful or picturesque about Wagner on the diamond. His movements have been likened to the gambols of a caracoling elephant. He is ungainly and so bowlegged that when he runs his limbs seem to be moving in a circle after the fashion of a propeller. But he can run like the wind.

NEW YORK AMERICAN. Nov. 19, 1907

One day he was batting against a young pitcher who had just come into the league. The catcher was a kid, too. A rookie battery. The pitcher threw Honus a curveball, and he swung at it and missed and fell down on one knee. Looked helpless as a robin. I was kind of surprised, but the guy sitting next to me on the bench poked me in the ribs and said, "Watch this next one." Those kids figured they had the old man's weaknesses, you see, and served him up the same dish—as he knew they would. Well, Honus hit a line drive so hard the fence in left field went back and forth for five minutes.

BURLEIGH GRIMES

Just pitch the ball and pray.

> JOHN MCGRAW, to pitcher who wanted to know how to pitch to Honus Wagner

---

Harry Walker

We'd be lounging in the Astro bullpen and Harry would call down to tell us to be alert so we could holler to our right fielder which base to throw to in the event he had to turn his back to get a ball off the wall. An important detail that could mean the ball game and only Harry Walker would think of it. Then we'd spend the rest of the game griping about what a pain Harry Walker was to interfere with our leisure time.

> JIM BOUTON

Paul Waner

He had to be a very graceful player, because he could slide without breaking the bottle on his hip.

CASEY STENGEL

Big Ed Walsh

[Charles Dryden described] Ed Walsh of the White Sox as the "only man in the world who can strut sitting down."

JONATHAN YARDLEY

Hoyt Wilhelm

I think catching Hoyt Wilhelm and his knucklers ruined my career. The more I caught him, the worse I got.

GUS TRIANDOS

Earl Williams

I mentioned Earl Williams as the worst [catcher] I ever threw to. I don't mean to knock the guy, and I know a lot of managers wanted him back there because he was such a good hitter, but from a pitcher's standpoint he was a disaster. The complete responsibility for calling a game was on your back; you had no help at all out there. He had no clue what to call when; it was like a random walk with him behind the plate.

TOM HOUSE

Ted Williams

All I want out of life is that when I walk down the street folks will say, "There goes the greatest hitter that ever lived."

TED WILLIAMS as a young player

. . . I went up and asked him, "What do I have to do to become a great hitter?"

He said, "Kid, I've seen you in batting practice. . . ." Now this is the great Lefty O'Doul, and I'm barely eighteen years old. He says, "You just keep doing exactly what you're doing and don't let anyone change you." Now that lifted me up to the heights!

And nobody ever did try to change me. Nobody!

TED WILLIAMS

But after I'd played in the American League one round, one series against each team, I said—and you know, I wasn't hitting that good, only about .260—but I said, "I don't see no blinding fastballs or exploding curves."

TED WILLIAMS

One of the remarkable things about him is that he never goes after a bad ball. He must have a wonderful pair of eyes. What's his weakness? I don't think he has anything approaching a weakness.

JIMMY FOXX

If ever a player deserved to hit. 400, it's Ted. He never sat down against tough pitchers. He never bunted. He didn't have the advantage of the sacrifice-fly rule like those hitters before him.

JOE CRONIN, after Williams had hit .406 in 1941

If the average player was going to bat four times in a game and got hits his first three times up, he'd be satisfied even if he failed the fourth time up. He'd relax after the third hit. Ted was his most vicious his fourth time up. That's what set him apart.

PUMPSIE GREEN

So that was Ted Williams. No use throwing at him. First of all, you're not going to hit him. And second of all, you're not going to bother him. Best thing to do with him was to let him do what he was going to do anyway and then concentrate on getting the next man out.

PAUL RICHARDS

Every third word out of Williams's mouth was a swear word. These adjectives were an absolutely essential part of his baseball vocabulary. One night, in Washington, President Nixon used our locker room as his ballpark office . . .

After the game [Nixon] paused to talk baseball with us. I was my usual delightful self, being smart enough not to mention football, and was in the middle of a wonderful story about me when Williams rapped on the door.

The four umpires in the room became so quiet you could have heard a stolen baseball drop.

The Secret Service agents brought Williams into the room. I knew exactly what was coming and closed my eyes, although that did not affect my hearing. "Hey," Williams said after being introduced to the President of the United States. "How the $&#* are you?"

Nixon didn't hesitate. He looked at the four of us and said, "Oh, don't worry about that. I've met the $&#*#$ before."

RON LUCIANO

Best hitter I ever saw? No, not Cobb, not Joe Jackson, not Babe Ruth. Teddy Williams. No question. He could do everything.

JIMMY DYKES

Jud Wilson

He faced the best of the whites—Lefty Grove, Dizzy Dean, and many others—and in 23 games he hit .330. It was an even .400 until age caught up with him.

"They all looked the same to me," Jud shrugged.

JOHN B. HOLWAY

Gene Woodling

I'd go to Catholic churches for Sunday services because they had early mass. I couldn't go to my church at eleven because I had to be at the ballpark. I was a Christian, but I didn't believe religion had a place at the ballpark. The Good Lord wasn't going to do any more for a religious batter than anyone else.

GENE WOODLING

Carl Yastrzemski

My first two years, when Carl Yastrzemski was up, if Carl didn't swing, it was not a strike. And I mean to tell you I threw balls right down the middle of the plate, belt-high, and you could not doubt it, but if Carl didn't swing, it was not a strike.

JACK MORRIS

Rudy York

The record book shows that, at one time or another during his thirteen seasons of major league baseball, Rudy York was an outfielder, a third baseman, and a catcher as well as a third baseman. If this suggests the adjective "versatile," it is misleading. No matter where he was stationed in the field, Rudy York always played the same position.

He played bat.

RED SMITH

Cy Young

A man who isn't willing to work from dreary morn till weary eve shouldn't think about becoming a pitcher.

CY YOUNG

Those Quoted

Unless otherwise noted, all years cited are for major leagues only.

Aaron, Henry: outfielder, 1954–1976; lifetime 755 home runs, 2297 RBI; Hall of Fame

Alexander, Charles C.: baseball historian, biographer

Alexander, Grover Cleveland: pitcher, 1911–1930; won 373 games; Hall of Fame

Algren, Nelson: novelist

Allen, Dick: outfielder, 1963–1977

Allen, Lee: sports writer, curator of Hall of Fame

Allen, Maury: baseball historian

Alou, Felipe: outfielder, 1960–1974; lifetime .307 hitter; coach, 1970s-1980s; manager 1992–

Alston, Walter: pitcher, 1936; manager 1954–1976; finished first seven times, won four World Series; Hall of Fame

Angell, Roger: author, editor

Aschburner, Steve: sportswriter

Ashburn, Richie: outfielder 1948–1962; lifetime .308 hitter, defensive star; Hall of Fame

Aulick, W. H.: newspaper sportswriter, early 20th century

Baer, Arthur (Bugs): columnist, 1920s–1940s

Barber, Red (Walter Lanier): sportscaster, author

Barnicle, Mike: sportswriter

Barrow, Ed: manager, 1903–1904, 1918–1920; won one pennant, one World Series; executive, 1917–1945; Hall of Fame

Barzun, Jacques: Romance Languages scholar

Baylor, Don: outfielder, 1970–1988; manager, 1993–1998; 2000; coach

Bell, Cool Papa (James): longtime star outfielder of Negro leagues; Hall of Fame

Bell, Les: infielder, 1923–31

Bench, Johnny: catcher, 1967–1983; 385 home runs; Hall of Fame

Benchley, Robert: humorist, 1920s–1940s

Berg, Moe (Morris): catcher, 1923–1939; multi-linguist; spy for OSS during World War II

Berra, Yogi (Lawrence): catcher, 1946–1965; 358 home runs; manager, 1964, 1972–1975, 1984–1985; coach; Hall of Fame

Blount, Roy, Jr.: sportswriter, humorist

Bluege, Ossie (Oswald): infielder, 1922–1939; manager, 1943–1947; coach

Bodie, Ping (Frank): outfielder, nine seasons, 1911–1921

Bonds, Barry: outfielder, 1986–

Boswell, Thomas: sportswriter

Bouton, Jim: pitcher, 1962–1970, 1978; author

Boyer, Clete (Cletis): infielder, 1955–1971

Bragan, Bobby: catcher, six seasons, 1941–1948; manager, 1956–1958, 1963–1966; coach

Breslin, Jimmy: columnist

Bridges, Rocky (Everett): infielder, 1951–1961; coach

Broeg, Bob: sportswriter

Brosnan, Jim: pitcher, nine seasons, 1954–1963; author; sportscaster

Bunning, Jim: pitcher, 1955–1971; 224 lifetime wins; Hall of Fame

Byrne, Tommy: pitcher, thirteen years, 1943–1957

Byron, Bill: longtime umpire, majors 1913–1919

Cannon, Jimmy: sportswriter

Chandler, Happy (Albert B.): Commissioner of Baseball, 1945–1951; U. S. Senator

Chandler, Spud (Spurgeon): pitcher, 1937–1947

Church, Seymour R.: sportswriter, late 19th: early 20th century

Cobb, Ty (Tyrus): outfielder, 1905–1928; lifetime batting average .366; led league in hitting twelve seasons; 892 stolen bases; manager, 1921–1926; Hall of Fame

Cochrane, Mickey: catcher, 1925–1937; .320 lifetime batting average; manager, 1934–1938; won two pennants, one World Series; Hall of Fame

Cohen, Marvin: author, teacher

Cohen, Morris R.: legal philosopher

Coleman, Jerry: infielder, 1949–1957; manager, 1980; sportscaster

Concepcion, Dave: infielder, 1970–1988

Coveleski, Stan: pitcher, sixteen seasons, 1912–1928; won 215 games; Hall of Fame

Crawford, Sam: outfielder, 1899–1917; 1,525 runs batted in; Hall of Fame

Creamer, Robert W.: sportswriter, biographer, editor

Cronin, Hep: scout

Cronin, Joe: infielder, 1926–1945; manager 1933–1947; won one pennant; general manager Red Sox, 1948–1959; president American League, 1959–1973; Hall of Fame

Crowther, Hal: sportswriter, columnist

Dandridge, Ray: star infielder, Negro leagues, 1933–1948; Hall of Fame

Danzig, Allison: sportswriter, author

Day, Leon: star pitcher of Negro leagues; Hall of Fame

De Maestri, Joe: infielder, 1951–1961

Dean, Dizzy (Jay Hanna): pitcher, 1930–1938; sportscaster; Hall of Fame

Deford, Frank: sportswriter

Dickey, Bill: catcher, 1928–1946; lifetime .313 hitter; manager, 1946; Hall of Fame

DiMaggio, Joe: outfielder, thirteen seasons, 1936–1948; .325 lifetime hitter; hit in 56 consecutive games, 1941; Hall of Fame

Doyle, Larry: infielder, 1907–1920

Drabowsky, Moe (Myron): pitcher, 1956–1972

Drysdale, Don: pitcher, 1956–69; 209 lifetime wins; sportscaster; Hall of Fame

Durocher, Leo: infielder, seventeen years, 1925–1945; manager, 24 years, 1939–1973; won three pennants, one World Series; Hall of Fame

Dykes, Jimmy: infielder, 1918–1939; manager, twenty-one seasons, 1934–1961

Einstein, Charles: sportswriter

Erskine, Carl: pitcher, 1948–1959

Evans, Billy: umpire, 1906–1927; Hall of Fame

Evers, Johnny: infielder, 1902–1917; "Tinker to Evans to Chance"; manager, 1913, 1921, 1924; Hall of Fame

Falkner, David: author, actor

Farrell, James T.: novelist

Feller, Bob: pitcher, seventeen seasons, 1936–1956; 266 lifetime wins; Hall of Fame

Finley, Charles O.: executive, Kansas City, Oakland, 1961–1980

Fischer, Bill: pitcher, 1956–1964; coach

Flood, Curt: outfielder, fifteen years, 1956–1971

Foster, Rube (Andrew): longtime Negro leagues pitcher, owner, league president; "The Father of Black Baseball"; Hall of Fame

Fowler, Art: pitcher, nine seasons, 1954–1964; coach

Fox, Charlie: manager, eight years, 1970–1976, 1983; coach

Foxx, Jimmy: infielder, catcher, 1925–1945; 534 lifetime home runs, .325 batting average; Hall of Fame

Freedman, Andrew: owner, New York Giants, 1895–1902; Tammany politico

Frick, Ford: sportswriter; president National League, 1934–1951; Commissioner of Baseball, 1951–1965; Hall of Fame

Frisch, Frank: infielder, 1919–1937; lifetime .316 hitter; manager, 16 years, 1933–1951; Hall of Fame

Gaetti, Gary: infielder, 1981–

Gallico, Paul: author

Garvey, Steve: infielder, 1969–1987

Gehrig, Lou: infielder, 1923–1939; 493 home runs, 1,990 runs batted in; played in 2130 consecutive games; Hall of Fame

Gehringer, Charlie: infielder, 1924–1942; Hall of Fame

Giamatti, A. Bartlett: university professor, president; president, National League, 1986–1989; Commissioner of Baseball, 1989–1992

Gibson, Bob: pitcher, 1959–1975; 251 games won; coach; Hall of Fame

Glavine, Tom: pitcher, 1987–

Gomez, Lefty (Vernon): pitcher, 1930–1943; Hall of Fame

Gooden, Dwight: pitcher, 1984–

Goodwin, Doris Kearns: historian, university professor

Goslin, Goose (Leon): outfielder, 1921–1938; .316 lifetime batting average; Hall of Fame

Gossage, Goose (Richard): pitcher, 1972–1994; 310 saves

Graham, Frank: sportswriter

Graney, Jack: infielder, 1908–1922

Green, Pumpsie (Elijah): infielder, 1959–1963

Greenberg, Hank: infielder, outfielder, twelve seasons, 1933–1947; 331 home runs, 1,276 RBI; Hall of Fame

Griffith, Clark: pitcher, twenty seasons, 1891–1914; manager 1901–1920; executive, Washington Senators, 1920–1955

Grimes, Burleigh: pitcher, 1916–1934; 270 lifetime wins; manager, 1937–1938; Hall of Fame

Grove, Lefty (Robert Moses): pitcher, 1925–1941; won 300 games, .680 winning percentage; Hall of Fame

Guthrie, Bill: umpire, nine seasons, 1913–1932

Gutman, Dan: sportswriter

Gwynn, Tony: outfielder, 1982– ; eight batting championships through 1998

Haak, Howie: scout

Hall, Donald: poet, baseball historian

Hall, Stephen S.: science and travel writer

Haller, Tom: catcher, 1961–1972

Hargrove, Mike: infielder, outfielder, 1974–1985; manager, 1991–

Harmon, William: poet, critic

Hayworth, Ray: catcher, fifteen seasons, 1926–1945

Hebner, Richie: infielder, 1968–1985

Henderson, Rickey: outfielder, 1979– ; 1,297 stolen bases through 1998

Herman, Babe: outfielder, 1926–1937, 1945

Herman, Billy: infielder, fifteen years, 1931–1947; manager, 1947, 1964–1966; coach; Hall of Fame

Hershiser, Orel: pitcher, 1983–

Hill, Art: sportswriter

Hoeffer, W. E.: sportswriter, 1900s–1910s

Holtzman, Jerome: sportswriter, editor

Holway, John B.: baseball historian

Honig, Donald: author

Hooper, Harry: outfielder, 1909–1925; Hall of Fame

Hornsby, Rogers: infielder, 1915–1937; .358 lifetime batting average; manager, fourteen seasons, 1925–1937, 1952–1953; Hall of Fame

House, Tom: pitcher, 1971–1978; coach; author

Howser, Dick: infielder, 1961–68; manager, 1980–1986; three first place finishes, won one World Series; coach

Hoyt, Waite: pitcher, 1918–1927; won 237 games lifetime; sportscaster; Hall of Fame

Hubbell, Carl: pitcher, 1928–1943; 253 wins lifetime; Hall of Fame

Huggins, Miller: catcher, 1904–1916; manager, 1913–1929; won six pennants, three World Series; Hall of Fame

Hunter, Catfish (Jim): pitcher, 1965–1979; won 224 games lifetime; Hall of Fame

Hutton, Tommy: infielder, twelve seasons, 1966–1979; sportscaster

Huyke, Woody: scout

Irvin, Monte: star in Negro leagues; infielder, outfielder, 1949–1956; Hall of Fame

Jackson, Reggie: outfielder, 1967–1987; 563 home runs; Hall of Fame

Jackson, Shoeless Joe: outfielder, 1908–1920; lifetime batting average .358; banned from game for lifetime in Black Sox scandal

Jennings, Hugh: infielder, seventeen seasons, 1891–1918; .311 lifetime batting average; manager, fourteen seasons, 1907–1920; three pennants; Hall of Fame

Jeter, Derek: infielder, 1995–

Johnson, Judy (William): star infielder of Negro leagues; Hall of Fame

Johnson, Walter: pitcher, 1907–1927; 416 lifetime victories; manager, 1929–1935; Hall of Fame

Kachline, Clifford: baseball historian, statistician

Kahn, Roger: sportswriter

Kaplan, Jim: sportswriter, author

Keeler, Wee Willie: outfielder, 1892–1909; lifetime batting average .341; Hall of Fame

Kell, George: infielder, 1943–1957; sportscaster; Hall of Fame

Kieran, John: columnist, essayist

Kiner, Ralph: outfielder, 1946–1955; 369 lifetime home runs; sportscaster; Hall of Fame

Kinsella, W. P.: novelist

Kissell, George: coach, 1969–1975; scout

Kluszewski, Ted: infielder, 1947–1961

Knoblauch, Chuck: infielder, 1991–

Koppett, Leonard: sportswriter, editor

Krich, John: novelist, sportswriter

Lardner, John: sportswriter, columnist

Lardner, Ring: sportswriter, author, humorist

LaValliere, Mike: catcher, 1984–1995

Leonard, Buck (Walter): star infielder in Negro leagues, 1933–1950; Hall of Fame

Lieb, Fred: sportswriter

Lindstrom, Fred: infielder, 1924–1936; .311 lifetime batting average; Hall of Fame

Lolich, Mickey: pitcher, 1963–1979; 217 lifetime wins

Lopat, Eddie: pitcher, 1944–1955; manager, 1963–1964

Lowe, QV: scout, coach

Lowry, Philip J.: baseball historian

Luciano, Ron: umpire, 1968–1980; author

Lyle, Sparky (Albert W.): pitcher, 1967–1982; 238 saves

Lyons, Ted: pitcher, twenty-one seasons, 1923–1946; 260 lifetime wins; Hall of Fame

Mack, Connie: catcher, 1886–1896; manager, 53 seasons, 1894–1950; won eight pennants, five World Series; Hall of Fame

Mantle, Mickey: outfielder, 1951–1968; 536 lifetime home runs; Hall of Fame

Maranville, Rabbit (Walter): infielder, 1912–1935; Hall of Fame

Marazzi, Rich: baseball columnist

Maris, Roger: outfielder, 1957–1968; broke Babe Ruth's record with 61 home runs in 1961 season

Marquard, Rube: pitcher, 1908–1926; Hall of Fame

Mathewson, Christy: pitcher, 1900–1916; won 373 games; manager 1916–1918; Hall of Fame

Mathis, Verdell: longtime pitching star in Negro leagues

Mathews, Eddie: infielder, 1952–1968; 512 lifetime home runs; manager 1972–1974; Hall of Fame

Mauch, Gene: infielder, nine seasons, 1944–1957; manager, 1960–1982, 1985–87

Mays, Carl: pitcher, 1915–1929; 208 lifetime wins

Mays, Willie: outfielder, 22 seasons, 1951–1973; 660 home runs; Hall of Fame

McCarthy, Eugene J.: U. S. Senator

McCarthy, Joe: manager, 24 seasons, 1926–1950; won nine pennants, seven World Series; Hall of Fame

McCarver, Tim: catcher, 1959–1980; sportscaster, sportswriter

McGraw, John: infielder, 1891–1906; .344 lifetime batting average; manager, 33 years, 1899–1932; won ten pennants, three World Series; Hall of Fame

McGraw, Tug (Frank): pitcher, 1965–1984

McGwire, Mark: infielder, 1986– ; set new record of 70 home runs in 1998

Meany, Tom: sportswriter, 1920s–1950s

Medwick, Joe: outfielder, 1932–1948; .333 lifetime batting average; Hall of Fame

Merrill, Durwood: umpire, 1977–

Miller, Ray: manager, 1985–1986, 1999; coach

Mills, Brad: infielder, 1980–1983

Moon, William Least Heat: authorMorris, Jack: pitcher, 1977–1994; 254 lifetime wins

Murdock, Eugene: baseball historian

Murray, Jim: baseball columnist, editor

Musial, Stan: outfielder, infielder, 22 seasons, 1941–1963; .331 lifetime batting average, 475 home runs; Hall of Fame

Nash, Ogden: poet

Nehf, Art: pitcher, 1915–1929

Newcombe, Don: pitcher, ten seasons, 1949–1960

Newsom, Bobo (Louis Norman): pitcher, twenty seasons, 1929–1953; won 222 games

O'Farrell, Bob: catcher, 1915–1935; manager, 1927, 1934

Oh, Sadaharu: Japanese baseball star; hit 858 home runs

Okrent, Dan: sportswriter

O'Loughlin, Silk (Francis): umpire, 1902–1918

O'Neil, Buck (John): star player, manager in Negro leagues; coach; scout

Owens, Paul: scout

Pafko, Andy: outfielder, 1943–1959

Page, Ted: outfield star of Negro leagues

Paige, Satchel (Leroy): pitching star and best-known player in Negro leagues; entered major leagues at age 42; pitcher, five years, 1948 -1953; Hall of Fame

Palmer, Jim: pitcher, nineteen seasons, 1965–1984; 268 lifetime wins; Hall of Fame

Pascarelli, Peter: sportswriter, baseball historian

Piersall, Jimmy: outfielder, seventeen seasons, 1950–1967

Piet, Tony: infielder, 1931–1938

Polner, Murray: author, biographer

Pryor, Greg: infielder, ten seasons, 1976–1986

Quigley, Martin: author

Radcliffe, Ted: longtime Negro leagues star; often pitched and caught doubleheaders

Rader, Doug: infielder, 1967–1977; manager, seven seasons, 1960s -1990s; coach

Reese, Pee Wee (Harold): infielder, sixteen seasons, 1940–1958; Hall of Fame

Rhodes, Dusty (James): outfielder, seven seasons, 1952–1959

Rice, Grantland: columnist, author, 1900s–1950s

Richards, Paul: catcher, 1932–1935, 1942–1946; manager, 1952–1961, 1976

Rickey, Branch: catcher, 1905–1907, 1914; manager, ten seasons, 1913–1925; executive, 1910s–1950s; pioneered in farm system; ended racial segregation in professional baseball; Hall of Fame

Ripken, Cal, Sr.: manager, 1986–1988; coach

Ritter, Lawrence: baseball historian, university professor

Roberts, Robin: pitcher, 1948–1966; won 245 games; Hall of Fame

Robinson, Jackie: infielder, 1947–1956; .311 lifetime batting average; in 1947 became the first black player in major leagues; Hall of Fame

Robinson, Wilbert: catcher, 1886–1902; manager, 1902, 1914–1931; Hall of Fame

Roe, Preacher (Elwin): pitcher, 1938, 1944–1954

Rogell, Billy: infielder, fourteen seasons, 1925–1940

Rolfe, Shelley: sportswriter, columnist

Rose, Pete: infielder, outfielder, 1963–1986; set lifetime records of 3,562 major league games played, 14,053 times at bat, 4,256 base hits; manager, 1984–1986; banned from baseball in 1989 for gambling

Roth, Philip: novelist

Roush, Edd: outfielder, eighteen seasons, 1911–1931; lifetime .323 batting average; Hall of Fame

Runyon, Damon: author, humorist

Ruppert, Jacob: owner, New York Yankees, 1915–1938

Ruth, Babe (George Herman): pitcher, outfielder, 1914–1935; hit 60 home runs in 1927; 714 home runs lifetime; lifetime .342 hitter; coach, 1938; Hall of Fame

Ryan, Blondy (John C.): infielder, six seasons, 1930–1938

Ryan, Nolan: pitcher, 1966, 1968–93; won 324 games, seven no-hitters, struck out 5,714 batters; Hall of Fame

Sain, Johnny: pitcher, 1942, 1946–1955; coach

Salter, Stephanie: sportswriter

Sauer, Hank: outfielder, 15 years, 1941–1959; coach

Sawyer, Eddie: managed 1948–1952, 1958–1960; won one pennant

Schecter, Leonard: sportswriter

Schmidt, Mike: infielder, 1972–1989; 542 lifetime home runs; Hall of Fame

Schumacher, Garry: sportswriter, publicist

Schupp, Ferdie: pitcher, 1913–1922

Seaver, Tom: pitcher, 1967–1986; 311 lifetime victories; Hall of Fame

Sewell, Joe: infielder, 1920–1933; lifetime .312 hitter; Hall of Fame

Shore, Ernie: pitcher, seven years, 1912 –1920

Shotton, Burt: outfielder, fourteen years, 1909–1923; manager, 1927–1934, 1947–1950; won two pennants; coach

Smelser, Marshall: baseball historian, biographer, university professor

Smith, Bob: pitcher, 1923–1937

Smith, Curt: sportswriter, baseball biographer

Smith, Red (Walter): columnist

Snider, Duke: outfielder, 1947–1967; 407 lifetime home runs; coach, 1974–1975; Hall of Fame

Snodgrass, Fred: outfielder, 1908–1916

Sosa, Sammy: outfielder, 1989–   ; hit 66 home runs in 1998

Spahn, Warren: pitcher, twenty-one seasons, 1942–1965; won 363 games lifetime; Hall of Fame

Spalding, Albert G.: pitcher, outfielder, 1871–1878; manager, 1876–1877; owner, 1882–1891; Hall of Fame

Speaker, Tris: outfielder, 1907–1927; 345 lifetime batting average; manager, 1919–1926; won one pennant, World Series

Stanky, Eddie: infielder, 1943–1953; manager, 1952–1955, 1966–1968, 1977; coach

Stargell, Willie: outfielder, infielder, 1962–1982; 475 home runs; coach; Hall of Fame

Stengel, Casey: outfielder, 1912–1925; manager, 1934–1943, 1949–1960, 1962–1965; won ten pennants, seven World Series, five in a row; coach; Hall of Fame

Stump, Al: sportswriter, biographer

Sullivan, Frank: pitcher, 1953–1963

Sunday, Billy: outfielder, 1883–1890; revivalist

Sutton, Don: pitcher, 1966–1988; 324 lifetime wins; sportscaster; Hall of Fame

Talese, Gay: author

Tenace, Gene: catcher, 1969–1983; coach

Terry, Bill: infielder, 1923–1936; lifetime .341 batting average; manager, 1932–1941; won three pennants, one World Series; Hall of Fame

Thomas, Frank: infielder, 1990–

Thome, Jim: infielder, 1991–

Tietje, Les: pitcher, 1933–1938

Triandos, Gus: catcher, 1953–1965

Van Slyke, Andy: outfielder, 1983–1995

Vaughn, Mo (Maurice): infielder, 1991–

Veeck, Mike: executive; son of Hall of Fame executive Bill Veeck

Verducci, Tom: sportswriter

Vick, Sam: outfielder, 1917–21; scout

Vincent, Fay: Commissioner of Baseball, 1989–1992

Voigt, David Quentin: baseball historian, university professor

Wagner, Honus (John Peter): infielder, 1887–1917; won eight batting championships, .327 lifetime average; coach; Hall of Fame

Walker, Rube (Albert): catcher, 1948–1958; coach

Wambganss, Bill: infielder, 1914–1926

Ward, Bruce: sportswriter

Ward, John Montgomery: pitcher, infielder, outfielder, 1878–1894; manager, seven seasons, 1880–1894; owner, 1912; Hall of Fame

Weaver, Buck (George): infielder, 1912–1920; banned from game for life in Black Sox scandal

Weaver, Earl: manager, 1968–1982, 1985–1986; six first-place finishes, won one World Series; Hall of Fame

Webb, Normal (Tweed): sportswriter, Negro leagues historian

Wells, Ed: pitcher, eleven seasons, 1923–1934

Werden, Percy: longtime player in Negro leagues

Wilhelm, Hoyt: pitcher, 1952–1972; won 123 games in relief; Hall of Fame

Wilkinson, J. L.: owner, Kansas City Monarchs

Will, George F.: columnist

Williams, Bernie: outfielder, 1991–

Williams, Dick: outfielder, 13 years, 1951–1964; manager, 1967–1988; six first place finishes, won three World Series

Williams, Joe: columnist, 1910s–1950s

Williams, Stan: pitcher, fourteen seasons, 1958–1972

Williams, Ted: outfielder, nineteen years, 1939–1960; .344 lifetime batting average, 521 homers; manager, 1969–1972; hit .406 in 1941; Hall of Fame

Wood, Smoky Joe: pitcher, outfielder, fourteen years, 1909–1922

Woodling, Gene: outfielder, seventeen seasons, 1943–1962; coach

Wright, Craig R.: sportswriter, baseball statistician

Wulf, Steve: sportswriter

Yardley, Jonathan: author, book critic

Young, Cy (Denton T.): pitcher, 1890–1911; won 511 games; pitched 7,356 innings; Hall of Fame

Zullo, Allen: sportswriter

Sources

Alexander, Charles C., *John McGraw.* New York: Viking Press, 1988.

Alexander, Charles C., *Our Game: An American Baseball History.* New York: Henry Holt, 1991.

Alexander, Charles C., *Rogers Hornsby: A Biography.* New York: Henry Holt and Co., 1995.

Allen, Lee, *Cooperstown Corner: Columns from The Sporting News, 1962–1969.* Cleveland, Ohio: Society for American Baseball Research, n.d.

Allen, Maury, *Baseball: The Lives behind the Seams.* New York: Macmillan Publishing Co., 1990.

Alvarez, Mark, "An Interview with Smoky Joe Wood," *Baseball Research Journal* [No. 16], 1987.

Angell, Roger, *Late Innings: A Baseball Companion.* New York: Simon and Schuster, 1982.

Angell, Roger, *Season Ticket: A Baseball Companion.* Boston: Houghton Mifflin, 1988.

Aschburner, Steve, "Beasts of Burden," *Street and Smith's Baseball* (March, 1999).

Bamberger, Michael, "Sammy: You're the Man," *Sports Illustrated,* 89, 13 (September 28, 1998).

Barber, Red, *The Rhubarb Patch: The Story of the Modern Brooklyn Dodgers.* New York: Simon and Schuster, 1954.

Barber, Red, *1947: When Hell Broke Loose in Baseball.* Garden City, N. Y.: Doubleday and Co., 1982.

Barber, Red, *Walk in the Spirit.* New York: The Dial Press, 1969.

Barber, Red, and Robert Creamer, *Rhubarb in the Catbird Seat.* Garden City, N. Y.: Doubleday and Co., 1968.

Baseball. Photographs by Walter Iooss, Jr.. Text by Roger Angell. New York: Harry N. Abrams, 1984.

Bax, Richard, *Ty Cobb: His Tumultuous Life and Times.* Dallas, Tex.: Taylor Publishing Co., 1994.

Benchley, Robert, *Love Conquers All.* New York: Henry Holt and Co., 1922.

Bethel, Dell, *Inside Baseball: Tips and Techniques for Coaches and Players.* Chicago: Henry Regnery Co., 1969.

Boswell, Thomas, *How Life Imitates the World Series: An Inquiry into the Game.* Garden City, N. Y.: Doubleday and Co., 1982.

Boswell, Thomas, *Why Time Begins on Opening Day.* Garden City, N. Y.: Doubleday and Co., 1984.

Boswell, Thomas, *The Heart of the Order.* New York: Doubleday and Co., 1989.

Bouton, Jim, *Ball Four: plus Ball Five.* New York: Stein and Day, 1981. [Ball Four orig. publ. 1970]

Bouton, Jim, with Neil Offen, "I Managed Good, But Boy Did They Play Bad." Chicago: Playboy Press, 1973.

Bready, James H., *The Home Team: 1859–1959, A Full Century of Baseball in Baltimore.* n.p., [1959].

Broeg, Bob, *The Pilot Light and the Gas House Gang.* St. Louis, Mo.: The Bethany Press, 1980.

Brosnan, Jim, *The Long Season.* New York: Penguin Books, 1983. [originally publ. 1960].

Cairns, Bob, *Pen Men: Baseball's Greatest Bullpen Stories Told by the Men Who Brought the Game Relief.* New York: St. Martin's Press, 1992.

Callahan, Gerry, "A Fall Classic," *Sports Illustrated,* 87, 13 (September 29, 1997).

Church, Seymour R., *Base Ball: The History, Statistics and Romance of the American National Game.* Vol. I. The 1902 Edition in Facsimile. Introduction by Brock Brower. Princeton, N. J.: The Pine Press, 1974.

Cobb, Ty, with Al Stump, *My Life in Baseball: The True Record.* Introduction by Charles C. Alexander. Lincoln: University of Nebraska Press, 1993. [orig. publ. 1961].

Cochrane, Gordon S. (Mickey), *Baseball: The Fan's Game.* Cleveland, Ohio: Society for American Baseball Research, 1992. [orig. publ. 1939].

Cohen, Marvin, *Baseball the Beautiful: Decoding the Diamond.* New York: Links Books, 1974.

Connor, Anthony J., *Baseball for the Love of It: Hall of Famers Tell It Like It Was.* New York: Macmillan Publishing Co., 1982.

Creamer, Robert W., *Babe: The Legend Comes to Life.* New York: Simon and Schuster, 1974.

Creamer, Robert W., *Baseball in '41: A Celebration of the "Best Baseball Season Ever"—in the Year America Went to War.* New York: Penguin Books, 1992.

Creamer, Robert W., *Mantle Remembered.* New York: Warner Books, 1995.

Creamer, Robert W., *Stengel: His Life and Times.* New York: Simon and Schuster, 1984.

Crowther, Hal, *Unarmed but Dangerous: Withering Attacks on All Things Phoney, Foolish, and Fundamentally Wrong with America Today.* Atlanta, Ga.: Longstreet Press, 1995.

Danzig, Allison, and Joe Reichler, *The History of Baseball: Its Great Players, Teams and Managers.* Englewood Cliffs, N. J.: Prentice-Hall, 1959.

Dittmar, Joe, "Tim Hurst," *The National Pastime.* No. 17 (1997).

Durocher, Leo, with Ed Linn, *Nice Guys Finish Last.* New York: Simon and Schuster, 1973.

Einstein, Charles, *Willie's Time: A Memoir.* New York: Berkley Books, 1979.

Farrell, James T., *My Baseball Diary.* New York: A. S. Barnes and Co., 1957.

Falkner, David, *The Short Season: The Hard Work and High Times of Baseball in the Spring.* New York: Times Books, 1986.

Feinstein, John, *Play Ball: The Life and Troubled Times of Major League Baseball.* New York: Villard, 1993.

Feldman, Jay, "Tweed Webb: He's Seen 'Em All," *Baseball Research Journal,* No. 18 (1989).

Fleming, G. H., *The Unforgettable Season.* Foreword by Lawrence Ritter. New York: Simon and Schuster, 1981.

Frommer, Harvey, *Baseball's Greatest Managers.* New York: Franklin Watts, 1985.

Frommer, Harvey, *Shoeless Joe and Ragtime Baseball.* Dallas, Tex.: Taylor Publishing Co., 1992.

Giamatti, A. Bartlett, *A Great and Glorious Game: Baseball Writings of A. Bartlett Giamatti,* edited by Kenneth S. Robson. Foreword by David Halberstam. Chapel Hill, N. C.: Algonquin Books of Chapel Hill, 1998.

Gmelch, George, and J. J. Winer, I*n the Ballpark: The Working Lives of Baseball People.* Washington, D. C.: Smithsonian Institution Press, 1998.

Graham, Frank, *The New York Giants: An Informal History.* New York: G. P. Putnam's Sons, 1952.

Grayson, Harry, "Honus Wagner," *NEA* feature story, 1943.

Grossinger, Richard, and Kevin Kerrane, ed., *Into the Temple of Baseball.* Berkeley, Calif.: Celestial Arts, 1990.

Gutman, Dan, *Baseball Babylon: From the Black Sox to Pete Rose, the Real Stories behind the Scandals that Rocked the Game.* New York: Penguin Books, 1992.

Hall, Donald, *Fathers Playing Catch with Sons: Essays on Sports* [Mostly Baseball]. San Francisco: North Point Press, 1985.

Holtzman, Jerome, ed., *No Cheering in the Press Box.* Rev. and expanded ed. New York: Henry Holt, 1995.

Holway, John B., *Blackball Stars: Negro League Pioneers.* Westport, Ct.: Meckler Books, 1988.

Holway, John B., *Josh and Satch: The Life and Times of Josh Gibson and Satchel Paige.* New York: Carroll and Graf Publishers/Richard Gallen, 1992.

Honig, Donald, *Baseball When the Grass Was Real: Baseball from the Twenties to the Forties Told by the Men Who Played It.* New York: Coward, McCann & Geoghegan, 1975.

Honig, Donald, *The Man in the Dugout: Fifteen Big League Managers Speak Their Minds.* Chicago, Ill.: Follett Publishing Company, 1977.

Honig, Donald, *The October Heroes: Great World Series Games Remembered by the Men Who Played Them.* New York: Simon & Schuster, 1979.

Honig, Donald, *The October Heroes: Great World Series Games Remembered by the Men Who Played Them.* New York: Simon and Schuster, 1979.

Irvin, Monte, with James A. Riley, *Nice Guys Finish First.* New York: Carroll and Graf, 1996.

Johnson, Dick, "A Conversation with Roger Angell," *SABR Review of Books,* III (1988).

Jordan, Pat, *The Suitors of Spring.* New York: Warner Paperback Library, 1974.

Kachline, Clifford, "Big Individual Performances Highlight Exciting '86 Season." *Official Baseball Guide: 1987 Edition.* St. Louis, Mo.: The Sporting News, 1988.

Kahn, Roger, *A Season in the Sun.* New York: Harper and Row, 1977.

Kahn, Roger, *The Boys of Summer*. New York: New American Library, 1973. [orig. publ. 1971].

Kaplan, Evan, "A Season to Remember," *Street and Smith's Baseball* (March, 1999).

Kaplan, Jim, *Pine-Tarred and Feathered: A Year on the Baseball Beat*. Chapel Hill, N. C.: Algonquin Books of Chapel Hill, 1985.

Kaplan, Jim, *Playing the Field*. Chapel Hill, N. C.: Algonquin Books of Chapel Hill, 1987.

Kerrane, Kevin, *Dollar Sign on the Muscle: The World of Baseball Scouting*. New York: Beaufort Books, 1984.

Kiersch, Edward, *Where Have You Gone, Vince DiMaggio?* New York: Bantam Books, 1983.

Kilgallen, James L., "Looking 'Em Over: New York Yankees," International News Service, 1939.

Koppett, Leonard, *All About Baseball*. New York: Quadrangle / New York Times Book Co., 1974.

Lardner, Ring W., *Some Champions: Sketches and Fiction*. ed. Matthew J. Bruccoli and Richard Layman. New York: Charles Scribner's Sons, 1976.

Lardner, Ring, W. *You Know Me Al: A Busher's Letters*. New York: Charles Scribner's Sons, 1960. (originally published 1916).

Lehmann-Haupt, Christopher, *Me and DiMaggio:* A Baseball Fan Goes in Search of His Gods. New York: Simon and Schuster, 1986.

Lieb, Fred, *Baseball As I Have Known It.* Foreword by Larry Ritter. New York: Coward, McCann and Geoghehan, 1977.

Lowry, Philip J., *Green Cathedrals.* Preface by Philip H. Bess. Cooperstown, N. Y.: Society for American Baseball Research, 1986.

Luciano, Ron, and David Fisher, *The Umpire Strikes Back.* Toronto and New York: Bantam Books, 1982.

Luciano, Ron, and David Fisher, *Remembrance of Swings Past.* New York: Bantam Books, 1988.

Lyle, Sparky, with Peter Golenbock, *The Bronx Zoo.* New York: Crown Books, 1979.

Maranville, Walter "Rabbit," *Run, Rabbit, Run: The Hilarious and Mostly True Tales of Rabbit Maranville.* Cleveland, Ohio: Society for American Baseball Research, 1991.

Marazzi, Rich, *The Rules and Lore of Baseball.* New York: Stein and Day, 1980.

Mathewson, Christy, *Pitching In a Pinch.* Introduction by Red Smith. New York: Stein and Day, 1977. [orig. publ. 1912, written by Jack Wheeler].

McCarver, Tim, with Danny Peary, *Tim McCarver's Baseball for Brain Surgeons and Other Fans: Understanding and Interpreting the Game So You Can Watch It like a Pro.* New York: Villard, 1998.

Murdock, Eugene, *Baseball Between the Wars: Memories of the Game by the Men Who Played It.* Westport, Ct.: Meckler Publishing, 1992.

Murdock, Eugene, *Baseball Players and Their Times: Oral Histories of the Game, 1920–1940.* Westport, Ct.: Meckler Publishing, 1991.

Murphy, J. M., *Napoleon Lajoie: Modern Baseball's First Superstar.* The National Pastime: A Review of Baseball History, Vol. VII, No. 1 (spring, 1988).

Nash, Bruce, and Allan Zullo, *The Baseball Hall of Shame,* 2. Bernie Ward, Curator. New York: Pocket Books, 1986.

Nemec, Raymond J., "The Performance and Personality of Percy Werden," *Baseball Research Journal,* 1977.

Okrent, Daniel, and Steve Wulf, *Baseball Anecdotes.* New York: Oxford University Press, 1989.

O'Neil, Buck, with Steve Wulf and David Conrads, *I Was Right on Time.* New York: Simon & Schuster, 1996.

Pascarelli, Peter, *The Toughest Job in Baseball: What Managers Do, How They Do It, and Why It Gives Them Ulcers.* New York: Simon and Schuster, 1993.

Peary, Daniel, ed., *We Played the Game: 65 Players Remember Baseball's Greatest Era, 1947–1964.* New York: Hyperion Books, 1996.

Polner, Murray, *Branch Rickey: A Biography.* New York: Atheneum, 1982.

Quigley, Martin, *The Crooked Pitch: The Curveball in American Baseball History.* Chapel Hill, N. C.: Algonquin Books of Chapel Hill, 1984.

Ritter, Lawrence S., *The Glory of Their Times: The Story of the Early Days of Baseball Told by the Men Who Played It.* New and enlarged ed. New York: William Morrow and Co., 1984.

Robinson, Ray, Matty—*An American Hero: Christopher Mathewson of the New York Giants.* New York: Oxford University Press, 1993.

Ruth, George Herman, *Babe Ruth's Own Book of Baseball.* Bison Books Introduction by Jerome Holtzman. Lincoln: Univ. of Nebraska Press, 1992. [orig. publ. 1928; written by Ford C. Frick].

Ryan, Nolan, with Mickey Herskovitz, *Kings of the Hill: An Irreverent Look at the Men on the Mound.* Hew York: Harper-Collins, 1992.

Smart, Steve, "Les Tietje," *The National Pastime: A Review of Baseball History,* No. 13 (1993).

Smelser, Marshall, *The Life That Ruth Built.* New York: Quadrangle / The New York Times Books, 1975.

Smith, Curt, *America's Dizzy Dean.* St. Louis, Mo.: The Bethany Press, 1978.

Smith, Red, *Press Box: Red Smith's Favorite Sports Stories.* New York: W. W. Norton, 1974.

Smith, Red, *To Absent Friends from Red Smith.* New York: Atheneum Publishers, 1982.

Solomon, Burt, *Where They Ain't: The Fabled Life and Untimely Death of the Original Baltimore Orioles, the Team that Gave Birth to Modern Baseball.* New York: The Free Press, 1999.

Spalding's Official Baseball Guide, 1937.

Spalding-Reach Official Base Ball Guide, 1941.

Stein, Fred, *Under Coogan's Bluff: A Fan's Recollections of the New York Giants under Terry and Ott.* Glenshaw, Pa.: Chapter and Cask, 1981.

Stump, Al, *Cobb: A Biography.* Chapel Hill, N. C.: Algonquin Books of Chapel Hill, 1994.

Sullivan, Dean A., ed., *Middle Innings: A Documentary History of Baseball,* 1900–1948. Lincoln: University of Nebraska Press, 1998.

Tarkach, Jim, "Stopping by Ballpark on a Snowy Evening," *The National Pastime: A Review of Baseball History*, 16 (1996).

Thorn, John, ed., *The Armchair Book of Baseball*. New York: Charles Scribner's Sons, 1985.

Thorn, John, Pete Palmer, Michael Gershman, David Pietrusza, and Dan Schlossberg, *Total Braves*. New York: Penguin Books, 1996.

Thorn, John, and Pete Palmer, *Total Baseball*. 2nd Edition. New York: Warner Books, 1991.

Thorn, John, Pete Palmer, Michael Gershman, and David Pietrusza, ed., *Total Baseball*. 6th ed. New York: Total Sports, Inc., 1999.

Verducci, Tom, "An Armful," *Sports Illustrated*, 87, 1 (July 7, 1997).

Verducci, Tom, "Triple Threats," *Sports Illustrated*, 85, 1 (July 1, 1996).

Voigt, David Quentin, *Baseball: An Illustrated History*. University Park: Pennsylvania State University Press, 1987.

Wallop, Douglas, *Baseball: An Informal History*. New York: W. W. Norton, 1969.

Ward, John Montgomery, *Base-ball: How to Become a Player, with the Origin, History, and Explanation of the Game*. Cleveland, Ohio: Society for American Baseball Research, 1993. [orig. publ. 1888].

Weaver, Earl, with Berry Stainback, *It's What You Learn After You Know It All That Counts.* Garden City, N.Y.: Doubleday and Co., 1982.

Will, George F., *Men at Work: The Craft of Baseball.* New York: Macmillan Publishing Co., 1990.

Williams, Peter, *When the Giants Were Giants: Bill Terry and the Golden Age of New York Baseball.* Chapel Hill, N. C.: Algonquin Books of Chapel Hill, 1994.

Williams, Peter, ed., *The Joe Williams Baseball Reader.* Chapel Hill, N. C.: Algonquin Books of Chapel Hill, 1989.

Williams, Ted, "It's Time to Open the Door," *The National Pastime: A Review of Baseball History,* No. 18 (1998).

Williams, Ted, with John Underwood, *The Science of Hitting.* New York: Simon and Schuster, 1971.

Wright, Craig R., and Tom House, *The Diamond Appraised.* New York: Simon and Schuster, 1989.

Yardley, Jonathan, *Ring: A Biography of Ring Lardner.* New York: Random House, 1977.

Zinsser, William, *Spring Training.* New York: Harper and Row, 1989.

Index

Y

Z